The Select Series: Microsoft® Windows® XP Brief Volume

Richard Alan McMahon, Sr.

Pamela R. Toliver
Series Editor

Upper Saddle River, New Jersey

LIBRARY OF CONGRESS CATALOGING-IN-PUBLICATION DATA

McMahon, Richard Alan.
    The select series. Microsoft Windows XP brief / Richard A. McMahon
      p. cm.
    ISBN 0-13-047252-2
    1. Microsoft Windows (Computer file) 2. Operating systems (Computers) I. Title.

QA76.76.O63 M39874 2002
005.4'469—dc21   2002009844

Publisher and Vice President: Natalie E. Anderson
Executive Acquisitions Editor: Jodi McPherson
Senior Project Manager: Thomas Park
Assistant Editor: Melissa Edwards
Editorial Assistant: Jasmine Slowik
Developmental Editor: Samantha Penrod
Media Project Manager: Cathleen Profitko
Marketing Manager: Emily Williams Knight
Production Manager: Gail Steier De Acevedo
Project Manager, Production: Tim Tate
Associate Director, Manufacturing: Vincent Scelta
Manufacturing Buyer: Natacha St. Hill Moore
Design Manager: Pat Smythe
Interior Design: Lorraine Castellano and Proof Positive/Farrowlyne Associates, Inc.
Cover Design: Lorraine Castellano
Full-Service Composition: Black Dot Group/An AGT Company
Printer/Binder: Banta Book Group, Menasha

Credits and acknowledgments borrowed from other sources and reproduced, with permission, in this textbook appear on the appropriate page within the text or at the end of the respective project.

Microsoft, Windows, Windows NT, MSN, The Microsoft Network, the MSN logo, PowerPoint, Outlook, FrontPage, and/or other Microsoft products referenced herein are either trademarks or registered trademarks of Microsoft Corporation in the U.S.A. and other countries. Screen shots and icons reprinted with permission from the Microsoft Corporation. This book is not sponsored by, endorsed by, or affiliated with Microsoft Corporation.

Copyright © 2002 by Prentice-Hall, Inc., Upper Saddle River, New Jersey, 07458. All rights reserved. Printed in the United States of America. This publication is protected by copyright and permission should be obtained from the publisher prior to any prohibited reproduction, storage in a retrieval system, or transmission in any form or by any means, electronic, mechanical, photocopying, recording, or likewise. For information regarding permission(s), write to: Rights and Permissions Department.

10 9 8 7 6 5 4 3 2 1
ISBN 0-13-047252-2

THE SELECT SERIES: MICROSOFT® OFFICE XP

Series Authors

Pamela R. Toliver and Yvonne Johnson

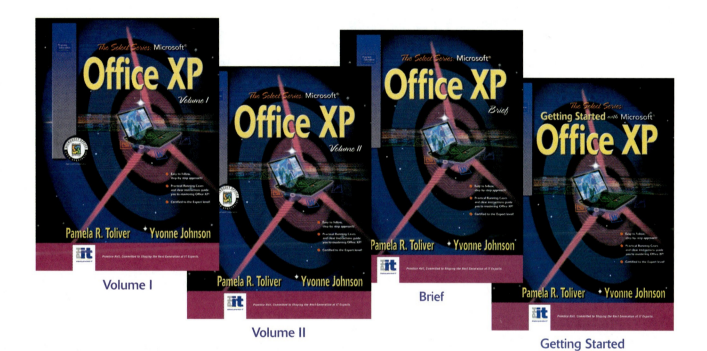

Volume I

Volume II

Brief

Getting Started

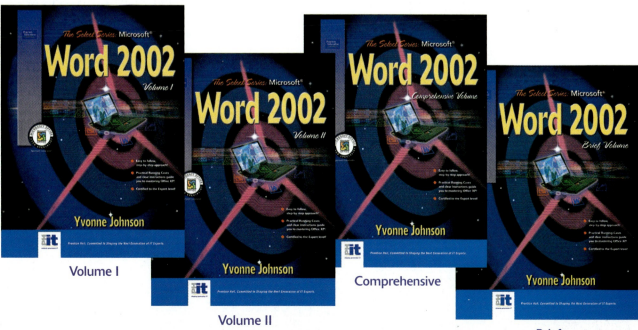

Volume I

Volume II

Comprehensive

Brief

Dedication

This textbook is dedicated to my family—my wife Sheronna, my daughter Lauren, and my son Ricky—because without their tolerance and assistance, it would never have happened.

Rich

Acknowledgments

I would like to acknowledge the extraordinary efforts of all those individuals involved in this project. It never ceases to amaze me just how hard the editors, copy editors, tech editors, development editors, project managers, marketing managers, compositors, publishers, printers, sales personnel, distributors, and campus book representatives (to name but a few) have to work in order to get a multi-faceted project like this into the hands of the reader. In particular, however, a special acknowledgment should go to the two people who took a chance and supported my desire to continue writing. Without their repeated personal support, I would not have worked on a project of this magnitude.

Lisa Lehman, who was the book representative for the UHD campus at the time, took a personal interest in getting fellow Houstonians writing for the company she represented. Lisa heard of my interest in writing additional textbooks and decided to champion my becoming a Prentice Hall author. She was persistent and continued searching upcoming projects until the right one surfaced. Then she presented the idea and even helped with the application process. Anyone who knows Lisa knows how tenacious she can be. This project's being offered to me is an outcome of that tenacity.

Jodi McPherson then decided to take a chance. The outcome of that chance is inside the cover of this textbook and the others of this series. Jodi is the one person who probably best knows all the bumps in the road that had to be overcome along the way to printing these texts. Without her backing this project would not have my name on it.

Hopefully, what you read will be worth the outstanding contributions of everyone involved.

Thank you, each and every one of you.

Rich

Preface

About this Series

The Select Series uses a class-tested, highly visual, project-based approach that teaches students through tasks using step-by-step instructions. You will find extensive full-color figures and screen captures that guide learners through the basic skills and procedures necessary to demonstrate proficiency in their use of each software application.

The Select Series introduces an all-new design for Microsoft Office XP. The easy-to-follow design now has larger screen shots with steps listed on the left side of the accompanying screen. This unique design program, along with the use of bold color, helps reduce distraction and keeps students focused and interested as they work. In addition, selectively placed Tip boxes and Other Ways boxes enhance student learning by explaining various ways to complete a task.

Our approach to learning is designed to provide the necessary visual guidance in a project-oriented setting. Each project concludes with a review section that includes a Summary, Key Terms & Skills, Study Questions, Guided Exercises, and On Your Own Exercises. This extensive end-of-project section provides students with the opportunity to practice and gain further experience with the tasks covered in each project.

What's New in the Select Series for Office XP

The entire Select Series has been revised to include the new features found in the Office XP suite, which contains Word 2002, Excel 2002, Access 2002, PowerPoint 2002, Publisher 2002, FrontPage 2002, and Outlook 2002.

The Select Series provides students with clear, concise instruction supported by its new design, which includes bigger screen captures. Steps are now located in the margin for ease of use and readability. This instruction is further enhanced by graded exercises in the end-of-project material.

Another exciting update is that every project begins with a Running Case from Selections, Inc., a department store that has opened shop online as e-Selections.com. Students are put in an e-commerce–based business environment so that they can relate what they are learning in Office XP to a real world situation. Everything is within a scenario that puts them in the department store where they perform tasks that relate to a particular division of the store or Web site.

About the Book

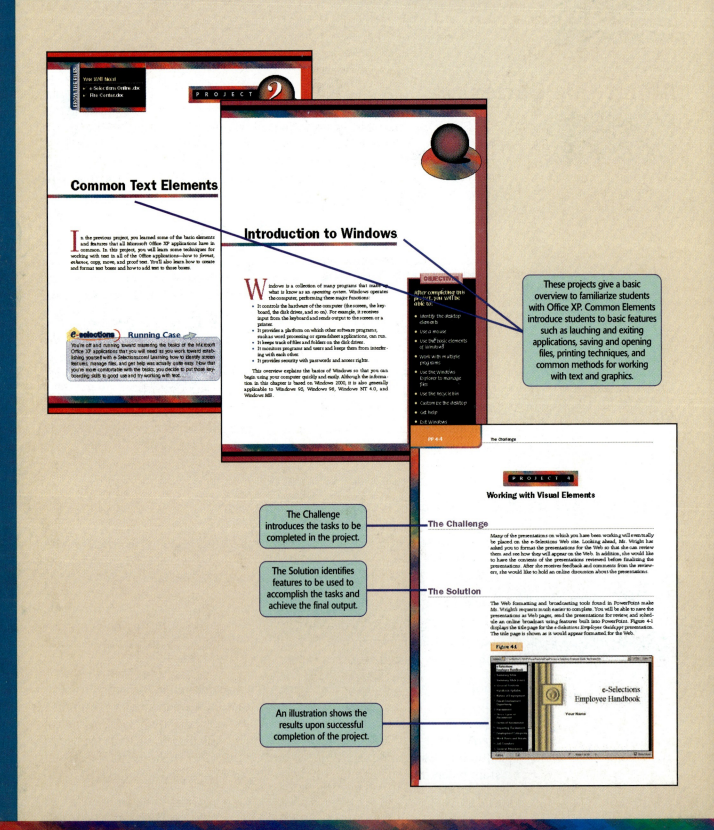

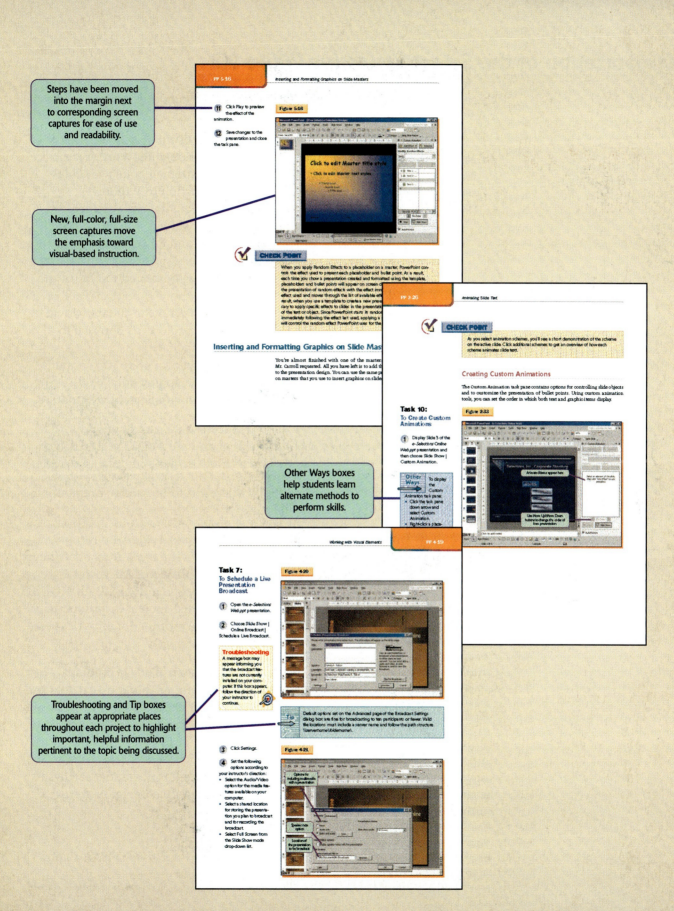

Organization of the Select Series for Office XP

The new Select Series for Office XP includes four combined Office XP texts from which to choose:

- **Microsoft Office XP Volume I** is MOUS certified at the Core level in each of the major applications in the Office suite (Word, Excel, Access, and PowerPoint). Four additional supplementary modules (Introduction to Internet Explorer, Introduction to Windows, Introduction to Outlook, and Common Elements) are also included. In addition, three integrated projects are included which integrate files and data among Word, Excel, Access, and PowerPoint.
- **Microsoft Office XP Volume II,** MOUS certified at the Expert level, picks up where Volume I leaves off, covering advanced topics for the individual applications.
- **Microsoft Office XP Brief** provides less coverage of the individual applications than Volume I (a total of four projects as opposed to six). The supplementary modules are also included.
- A new volume, **Getting Started with Microsoft Office XP,** contains the Introduction and first chapter from each application (Word, Excel, Access, and PowerPoint) plus the four supplementary modules.

Individual texts for Word 2002, Excel 2002, Access 2002, and PowerPoint 2002 provide complete coverage of each application and are MOUS certified. They are available in Volume I and Volume II texts and also as Comprehensive texts.

This series of books has been approved by Microsoft to be used in preparation for Microsoft Office User Specialist exams.

APPROVED COURSEWARE

The Microsoft Office User Specialist (MOUS) program is globally recognized as the standard for demonstrating desktop skills with the Microsoft Office suite of business productivity applications (Microsoft Word, Microsoft Excel, Microsoft PowerPoint, Microsoft Access, and Microsoft Outlook). With MOUS certification, thousands of people have demonstrated increased productivity and have proved their ability to utilize the advanced functionality of these Microsoft applications.

Customize the Select Series with Prentice Hall's Custom Binding program. The Select Series is part of the Custom Binding Program, enabling instructors to create their own texts by selecting projects from Office XP to suit the needs of a specific course. An instructor could, for example, create a custom text consisting of the specific projects that he or she would like to cover from the entire suite of products. The Select Series is part of PHit's Value Pack program in which multiple books can be shrink-wrapped together at substantial savings to the student. A value pack is ideal in courses that require complete coverage of multiple applications.

Instructor and Student Resources

Instructor's Resource CD-ROM

The **Instructor's Resource CD-ROM** that is available with the Select Office XP Series contains:

- Student data files
- Solutions to all exercises and problems
- PowerPoint lectures
- Instructor's manuals in Word format that enable the instructor to annotate portions of the instructor manual for distribution to the class
- A Windows-based test manager and the associated test bank in Word format

Companion Website www.prenhall.com/select

This text is accompanied by a companion Website at *www.prenhall.com/select*.

Features of this new site include the ability for you to customize your homepage with real-time news headlines, current events, exercises, an interactive study guide, student data files, and downloadable supplements. This site is designed to take learning Microsoft Office XP with the Select Series to the next level.

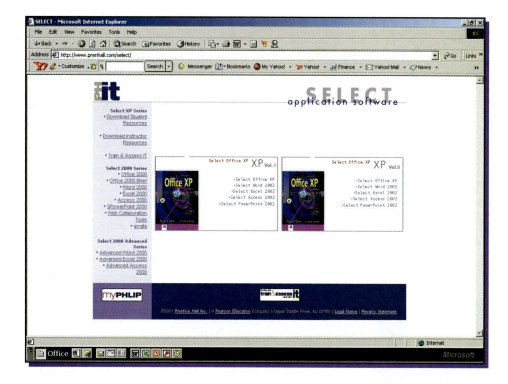

Now you have the freedom to personalize your own online course materials!
Prentice Hall provides the content and support you need to create and manage your own online course in WebCT, Blackboard, or Prentice Hall's own Course Compass. Choose "Standard" content to enhance the material from this text or "Premium" content, which provides you with even more lecture material, interactive exercises, and projects.

Training and Assessment   www.prenhall.com/phit

Prentice Hall offers Performance Based Training and Assessment in one product, Train&Assess IT. The Training component offers computer-based training that a student can use to preview, learn, and review Microsoft Office application skills. Web- or CD-ROM delivered, Train IT offers interactive, multimedia, computer-based training to augment classroom learning. Built-in prescriptive testing suggests a study path based not only on student test results but also on the specific textbook chosen for the course.

The Assessment component offers computer-based testing that shares the same user interface as Train IT and is used to evaluate a student's knowledge about specific topics in Word, Excel, Access, PowerPoint, Windows, Outlook, and the Internet. It does this in a task-oriented environment to demonstrate proficiency as well as comprehension of the topics by the students. More extensive than the testing in Train IT, Assess IT offers more administrative features for the instructor and additional questions for the student.

Assess IT also allows professors to test students out of a course, place students in appropriate courses, and evaluate skill sets.

CourseCompass   www.coursecompass.com

CourseCompass is a dynamic, interactive online course-management tool powered exclusively for Pearson Education by Blackboard. This exciting product allows you to teach market-leading Pearson Education content in an easy-to-use, customizable format.

BlackBoard   www.prenhall.com/blackboard

Prentice Hall's abundant online content, combined with Blackboard's popular tools and interface, result in robust Web-based courses that are easy to implement, manage, and use—taking your courses to new heights in student interaction and learning.

WebCT   www.prenhall.com/webct

Course-management tools within WebCT include page tracking, progress tracking, class and student management, gradebook, communication, calendar, reporting tools, and more. GOLD LEVEL CUSTOMER SUPPORT, available exclusively to adopters of Prentice Hall courses, is provided free-of-charge upon adoption and provides you with priority assistance, training discounts, and dedicated technical support.

Brief Table of Contents

Preface	**v**
Introducing Windows XP Professional	**WN-1**
Project 1: Windows XP Professional Basics	**WN 1-1**
Project 2: Working with Files and Folders	**WN 2-1**
Glossary	**WN G-1**
Index	**WN I-1**

Table of Contents

Preface	**v**
Introducing Windows XP Professional	**WN-1**
THE CHALLENGE	WN-2
THE SOLUTION	WN-2
Booting Up the Computer and Logging On Windows XP	**WN-2**
Task 1: To Boot the Computer and Log On Windows XP	WN-3
Identifying Desktop Features	**WN-5**
Using the Mouse on the Desktop	**WN-5**
Task 2: To Use the Mouse on the Desktop	WN-6
Displaying and Using the Start Menu	**WN-8**
Task 3: To Display and Use the Start Menu	WN-9
Displaying Cascading Submenus	**WN-10**
Task 4: To Display Cascading Submenus	WN-10
Identifying Dialog Box Features	**WN-11**
Changing Mouse Settings	**WN-12**
Task 5: To Change Mouse Settings	WN-12
Logging Off Windows XP	**WN-14**
Task 6: To Log Off Windows XP	WN-15
Summary and Exercises	**WN-16**
SUMMARY	WN-16
KEY TERMS	WN-17
SKILLS	WN-17
STUDY QUESTIONS	WN-18
Multiple Choice	WN-18
Short Answer	WN-19
Fill in the Blank	WN-19
For Discussion	WN-20

Project 1 Windows XP Professional Basics	**WN 1-1**
THE CHALLENGE	WN 1-2
THE SOLUTION	WN 1-2
Changing the Desktop Background	**WN 1-2**
Task 1: To Change the Desktop Background	WN 1-3
Creating File and Folder Objects	**WN 1-4**
Task 2: To Create File and Folder Objects	WN 1-5
Working with Folders	**WN 1-7**
Task 3: To Work with Folders	WN 1-8
Using the Recycle Bin	**WN 1-9**
Task 4: To Change Recycle Bin Settings	WN 1-10
Task 5: To Delete and Restore Recycle Bin Items	WN 1-13
Changing User Options	**WN 1-14**
Task 6: To Change User Options	WN 1-15
Switching Users and Shutting Down Windows XP	**WN 1-18**
Task 7: To Switch Users and Shut Down Windows XP	WN 1-19
Summary and Exercises	**WN 1-21**
SUMMARY	WN 1-21
KEY TERMS	WN 1-22
SKILLS	WN 1-22
STUDY QUESTIONS	WN 1-22
Multiple Choice	WN 1-22
Short Answer	WN 1-23
Fill in the Blank	WN 1-23
For Discussion	WN 1-24
GUIDED EXERCISES	WN 1-24
ON YOUR OWN	WN 1-26
Project 2 Working with Files and Folders	**WN 2-1**
THE CHALLENGE	WN 2-2
THE SOLUTION	WN 2-2
Using Files and Folders	**WN 2-2**
Task 1: To Use File and Folder Tools	WN 2-3
Task 2: To Change Folder Views in My Documents	WN 2-7
Task 3: To Manipulate Files and Folders	WN 2-9
Task 4: To Delete and Restore Files and Folders	WN 2-12

Working with Windows — WN 2-15
Task 5: To Work with Windows — WN 2-15

Switching Between My Computer and Windows Explorer Views — WN 2-18
Task 6: To Switch Between My Computer and Windows Explorer Views — WN 2-18

Navigating in Windows Explorer — WN 2-21
Task 7: To Navigate in Windows Explorer — WN 2-21

Customizing the Start Menu — WN 2-23
Task 8: To Customize the Start Menu — WN 2-23

Gathering Hard Drive Details — WN 2-26
Task 9: To Gather Hard Drive Details — WN 2-26

Conducting a Basic Search — WN 2-27
Task 10: To Conduct a Basic Search — WN 2-28

Formatting a Floppy Disk — WN 2-29
Task 11: To Format a Floppy Disk — WN 2-30

Summary and Exercises — WN 2-33
- **SUMMARY** — WN 2-33
- **KEY TERMS** — WN 2-34
- **SKILLS** — WN 2-34
- **STUDY QUESTIONS** — WN 2-34
  - Multiple Choice — WN 2-34
  - Short Answer — WN 2-35
  - Fill in the Blank — WN 2-35
  - For Discussion — WN 2-36
- **GUIDED EXERCISES** — WN 2-36
- **ON YOUR OWN** — WN 2-39

Glossary — WN G-1

Index — WN I-1

Introducing Windows XP Professional

When you work with Windows XP, you will notice that it is different from previous versions of the Windows operating system. The bright screen colors and modern graphics that are part of the user interface are designed to make the operating system easier to use. In this project, you will explore some of the fundamental features necessary for working with Windows XP.

OBJECTIVES

After completing this project, you will be able to:

- Boot up the computer and log on Windows XP
- Identify desktop features
- Use the mouse on the desktop
- Display and use the Start menu
- Display cascading submenus
- Identify dialog box features
- Change mouse settings
- Log off Windows XP

e-selections Running Case

As a recently hired administrative assistant in the e-Selections division of Selections, Inc., you have been trying to progress from answering the phones and sorting mail to actually performing some of the administrative functions the company needs. Months of careful planning have led the Information Technology (IT) department to select Windows XP Professional as the operating system for the company's new computers, and now they need someone to report on the new features of Windows XP.

Introducing Windows XP Professional

The Challenge

For the past three months, you have worked for Amber Wright, who seems pleased with your progress as her administrative assistant. Now she has offered you a new position as executive assistant and assigned you to one of the vacant offices. In addition to the promotion, you will receive one of the first workstations operating Windows XP. Your first assignment is to explore the features of Windows XP so you can relate information about the operating system to Ms. Wright.

The Solution

Although you are excited about the new job assignment, you are anxious about learning the intricacies of a new operating system. By learning Windows XP to satisfy your own job functions, you will prepare yourself to provide Ms. Wright with the information she needs. Because you are already familiar with other Windows operating systems, you can jump right in and log on, identify desktop features, use the Start menu and its cascading menus and dialog boxes, use the mouse and change its settings, and activate the log off procedure.

Booting Up the Computer and Logging On Windows XP

Windows XP starts automatically each time you turn on your computer. Depending on the setup of your computer system, it may be necessary to *log on* to a network or select your user account. A *user account* consists of a user name and *password* that you type for access to the Windows XP *desktop*.

In lab settings where the computers are left running, a *screen saver*—a constantly moving graphic or other item—helps preserve monitor resolution when there is no activity on the computer for extended periods of time. When a screen saver is active, you can access the Windows XP desktop (your onscreen workspace) by waking the computer. This displays the *Windows Welcome screen*, which provides a list of authorized users from which you can then log on using your user name.

Task 1:
To Boot the Computer and Log On Windows XP

1 Move the mouse. This should wake the computer if your system is turned on. If not, turn on the computer and monitor.

2 If necessary, log on to the network (ask your instructor if you need further directions). The Windows Welcome screen displays.

3 Click the link containing your user name. If a password has been assigned, you see a password entry box.

Figure 0-1

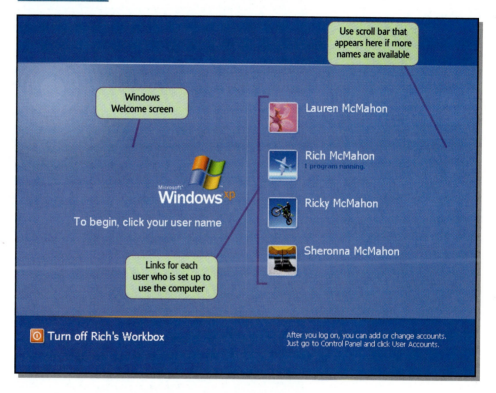

 Troubleshooting Some installations of Windows XP are set up such that users log on without typing a password. If no password is required, the Windows desktop appears when you click your user name. If no password is required on your computer, skip to Step 5 of this task.

4 Type your password in the Password entry box and press Enter to display the desktop.

To submit a password:
- Click the green arrow button beside the password entry box.

Password text is represented by dots to keep others from viewing your password. In Windows XP, passwords are *case sensitive*. Therefore, you must enter the exact combination of uppercase and lowercase characters used when the password was created.

5 Review the features of the desktop.

Figure 0-2

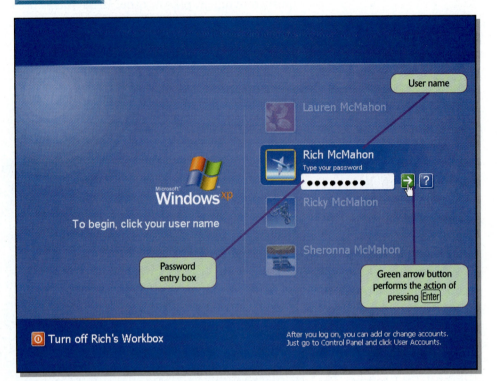

Figure 0-3

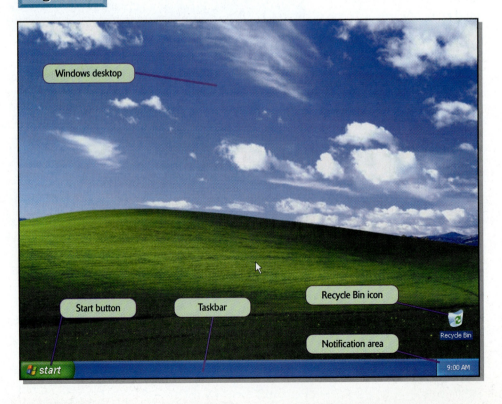

Identifying Desktop Features

While your desktop may be customized to incorporate tools unique to your lab, school, or workplace, a number of desktop features are common to all Windows XP installations. These features are displayed in Figure 0-3 and are identified in Table 0-1.

> **Tip** The notification area of the taskbar was called the taskbar tray or the system status tray in previous versions of Windows.

Table 0-1	Windows XP Desktop Features
Feature	**Description**
Desktop	A computer's onscreen rendition of the top of a desk. Objects placed on the desktop may be opened or moved.
Recycle Bin	An icon on the desktop that functions as a trash can. It stores items such as files, graphics, and so forth that the user deletes. Items in the Recycle Bin may be retrieved and restored when necessary but only prior to emptying the Recycle Bin.
Taskbar	The taskbar is the horizontal bar usually displayed at the bottom of the screen that holds items such as the Start button and taskbar buttons that identify computer tools in use.
Start button	One of the main mechanisms used to access applications and other computer tools. By default, the *Start button* is located on the lower left corner of the desktop—at the left end of the taskbar.
Taskbar button	A button on the taskbar that identifies programs that are running or files that are being used.
Notification area	The area on the far right side of the taskbar that holds icons representing available utility tools, such as the clock, volume adjustment, or power settings. These icons serve as shortcuts that you can use to open the available utility programs.

Using the Mouse on the Desktop

Because the Windows XP desktop is a *graphical user interface* (*GUI*) that incorporates modern, up-to-date features in a graphic environment using visual items such as tools, buttons, icons, and bars, a pointing device such as a *mouse* is essential. Common mouse terms and techniques are described in Table 0-2.

Tip Windows XP often highlights objects when you point to them and sometimes displays pop-up information boxes called pop-up descriptions when you pause the pointer over the object.

 Tip Pop-up descriptions in Windows XP are commonly referred to as Tool-tips in most Windows applications.

Table 0-2	Mouse Actions
Action	**Description**
Point	Move the mouse across the mouse pad or desk so the onscreen mouse pointer touches or points to the object with which you wish to work.
Pause	Hold the mouse pointer over a link or object for a few seconds to activate an informative message—a *pop-up description* (if one is associated with that link or object). This action is sometimes referred to as *hovering*.
Click	Press and release the left mouse button quickly. Use this action to select an object or to position an insertion point at a specific location.
Drag	Point at an object, press and hold the applicable mouse button down while you move the object to another location.
Double-click	Press and release the left mouse button twice in rapid succession. Use this action after pointing at an object to execute a command, such as launching an application or opening a file.
Triple-click	Press and release the left mouse button three times in rapid succession. Use this action to highlight a block of text, such as a paragraph.
Right-click	Press and release the right mouse button. Use this action to activate a context-sensitive menu, called a *shortcut menu*, of commands that apply to the object.

Task 2:
To Use the Mouse on the Desktop

1 Point to the bottom left corner of your desktop.

 Tip Moving your mouse lets you find where your mouse pointer is located, and moving the pointer to the lower left corner of the desktop simply gives you a convenient starting point for this task.

2 Move the mouse pointer in one quick diagonal motion and end at the upper right corner of the desktop.

Figure 0-4

Introducing Windows XP Professional   WN-7

3 Point to the **Recycle Bin** icon, drag the icon to the center of the desktop, and release the mouse button to position the icon in the center of the desktop.

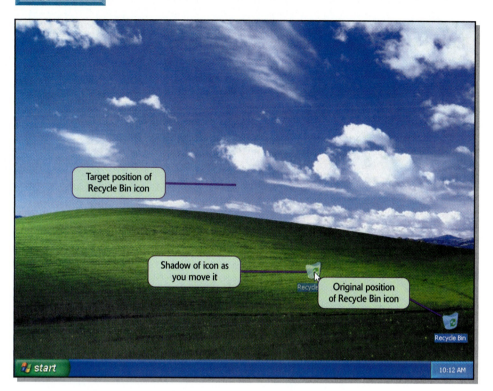

Figure 0-5

4 Right-click the taskbar to display the shortcut menu.

5 Click a blank area of the desktop to close the shortcut menu.

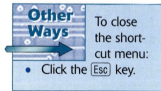

To close the shortcut menu:
- Click the [Esc] key.

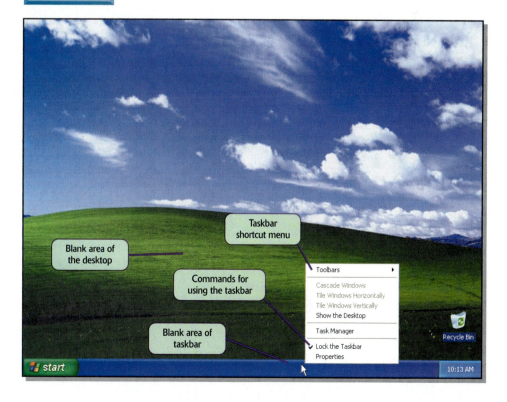

Figure 0-6

Displaying and Using the Start Menu

When you click the green Start button at the left end of the taskbar, the Start menu displays. The *Start menu* provides access to tools for launching programs, opening folders, searching your computer, requesting help, and much more. As you explore and use the Start menu, you will notice some features common to menus in Windows XP. These features are identified and described in Table 0-3.

Table 0-3	Windows XP Start Menu Features
Feature	**Description**
Start button	Used to display the Start menu.
User name	Identifies the currently logged-in user.
User picture	Picture chosen to represent the user.
Pinned area	Area where the default browser and e-mail programs in use are always listed. You can add additional pinned items to this area.
Separator lines	Dividers used to group similar types of items together.
Recent applications area	Location for shortcuts to the most recently used programs (applications).
Cascade arrow	Identifies an item that displays additional menus that cascade beside the active menu. In the default configuration, cascade arrows can be green (All Programs), blue (on the Start menu), or black (on subsequent submenus).
Ellipsis	Three dots that appear to the right of a menu item identifying it as one that will open with applicable *dialog boxes*.
Log Off button	The small yellow-brown button with a diagonal key symbol that opens the Log Off Windows dialog box.
Turn Off Computer button	The small red button with the power-off symbol. Used to initiate one of the procedures Windows XP must undertake prior to shutting down.

Task 3:
To Display and Use the Start Menu

1. Click the **Start** button on the taskbar to display the Start menu.

Other Ways

To open the Start menu:
- Press and hold down the Ctrl key and then press the Esc key.
- Press the ⊞ key.

2. Click the **Start** button again to close the Start menu. Then press the ⊞ key to redisplay the Start menu.

Tip The ⊞ key (*Windows Logo key*) is located between the Ctrl key and the Alt key on the left side of the keyboard.

3. Point to **All Programs** to display a cascading list of programs installed on your computer.

4. Click the **Start** button to close the Start menu.

Troubleshooting

By default, programs are initially grouped by type and listed on the All Programs list alphabetically. If the list on your computer is arranged in a different order, right-click anywhere on the list and select Sort by Name to change the order.

Figure 0-7

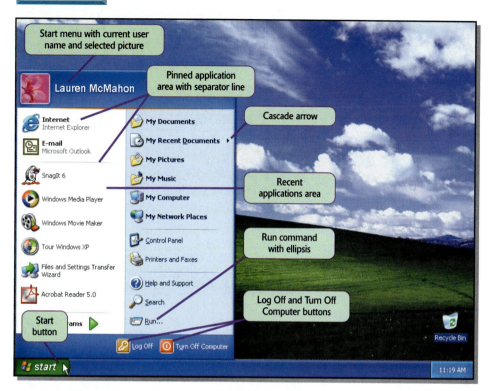

Figure 0-8

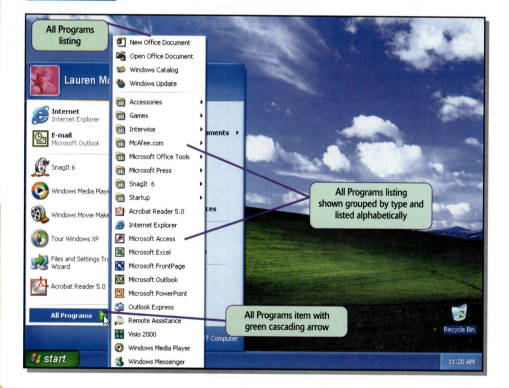

Other Ways

To display the All Programs list:
- Press the ⊞ key, press [P], and then press [→]. (If other items on your Start menu begin with the letter P, you may need to press [P] more than once to highlight the All Programs option.)

Displaying Cascading Submenus

Small, right-pointing triangular arrowheads that appear on menus such as the Start menu identify items that display additional cascading menus. You can explore these cascading submenus by selecting the Start menu items available through the All Programs cascading menu.

Because of system customizations, the programs shown on your computer may be different from those shown in the figures.

Task 4:
To Display Cascading Submenus

1 Display the Start menu and point to the **All Programs** green arrow.

2 Point to the **Accessories** menu item to display the Accessories menu with its listed Accessories programs and additional Accessories folders.

3 Point to **Communications** on the Accessories menu to display another cascading menu. Click a blank spot anywhere on the desktop to clear the selected menus from your screen.

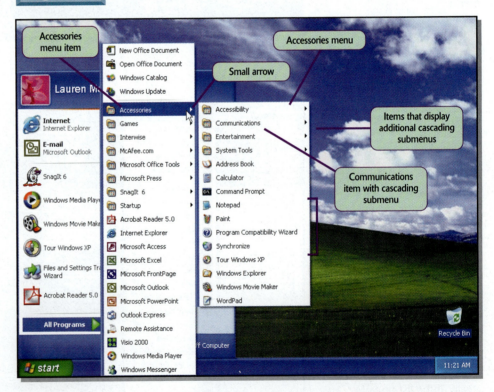

Figure 0-9

Tip Cascading menus appear to the right of the active menu as long as the full menu can appear on screen. When menu width exceeds monitor width, the cascading menus appear to the left of the active menu.

Identifying Dialog Box Features

As you have already noticed, some items on the Start menu appear with ellipses following the command name. These ellipses identify a command on a menu that opens a dialog box. A dialog box is a small window that contains options and settings to control different objects and features. Common dialog box features are identified and described in Table 0-4.

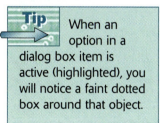 **Tip** Because dialog boxes display tools for setting options and controlling the behavior of different Windows XP features, the types of items that appear in dialog boxes vary. As a result, you will not always see each of the features described in Table 0-4 in all dialog boxes.

Tip When an option in a dialog box item is active (highlighted), you will notice a faint dotted box around that object.

Table 0-4	Dialog Box Features
Feature	**Description**
Title bar	The top blue band that contains the dialog box name on the left and the Help or navigation buttons such as the Close button on the right.
Help button	The blue question mark button on the right side of the title bar that is used to request context-sensitive assistance from Windows XP.
Close button	The red X button on the right side of the title bar that cancels your changes and closes the dialog box.
Text box	A white box used to enter text and other descriptive information.
OK button	A command button that implements the setting changes and closes the dialog box.
Cancel button	A command button that discards setting changes and closes the dialog box.
Browse button	A command button that opens the Browse dialog box, so you can search the computer for a file.
Drop-down list box	Provides a list of commands or options from which you can choose.
Pane (or panel or area)	A section of a dialog box that contains related information.
Option button	A small round item used to turn a feature on or off by placing (or removing) a dot in the circlelike image. The option button is activated by clicking it. Only one option button in each group of options can be active at any given time.
Check box	A square box used to turn a feature on or off by placing (or removing) a check mark in the boxlike image. The check box is activated (or cleared) by clicking it. Multiple items in each group of check boxes can be active at the same time.
Spin box	A small numeric or date entry item with an up and down arrow component. Clicking the arrow increases or decreases the entered information accordingly.
Dialog box tab	A small tab at the top of a dialog box used to change which page is being viewed when there are multiple pages of information available. Clicking the appropriate tab opens the applicable information page.

Changing Mouse Settings

Windows XP offers a variety of settings you can change to control the way the mouse acts on your computer. Adjusting these settings here is a great way to explore dialog box features. People who operate the mouse with the left hand can reverse the mouse buttons so they operate correctly with the left hand. Other options include changing the double-click speed and the shape of the mouse pointer.

Keystrokes enable you to issue commands and make selections in a dialog box without using the mouse. Although the mouse is often the most efficient tool for working with dialog boxes and menus, keystrokes are an alternative tool. Some keystroke commands are issued by combining a control or alternate key with the underlined characters in menu names, commands, and options. In this book, keyboard commands are represented by keycaps such as $\boxed{C}$. When a control or alternate key is required to issue the command, it is represented by a keycap followed by a plus sign (+) and the key name, such as $\boxed{Ctrl}$ + $\boxed{C}$. When you see this designation for a key combination, you execute the command by pressing and holding down the first key while you then press the second key.

Task 5:
To Change Mouse Settings

1. Display the Start menu.

2. Click **Control Panel** to open the Control Panel window.

> **Tip** When you open the Start menu by pressing the 🪟 key instead of clicking on the Start button, you see an underlined C in the Control Panel menu item. With the Start menu open, you can press $\boxed{C}$ to select the Control Panel option.

Figure 0-10

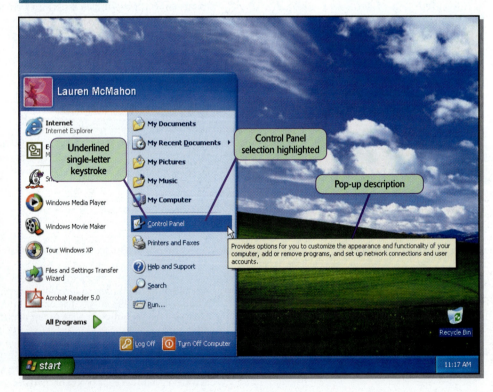

3 Click the **Printers and Other Hardware** icon to open the Printers and Other Hardware window.

> **Tip** In the top section of the window, you see the *title bar*, the *menu bar*, the *toolbar*, and the *address bar*. The title bar contains the control menu icon, the name of the document and/or application, and the Minimize, Maximize/Restore, and Close buttons. The menu bar provides access to menu commands. The toolbar consists of a row of toolbar buttons (icons), which allow you to perform common tasks quickly. The address bar provides a drop-down list that can be used to access or search for resources.

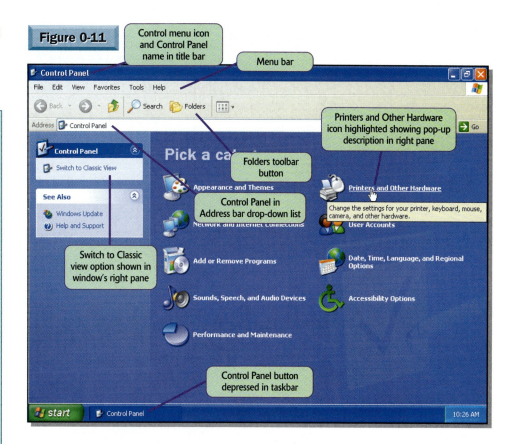

Figure 0-11

- Control menu icon and Control Panel name in title bar
- Menu bar
- Folders toolbar button
- Printers and Other Hardware icon highlighted showing pop-up description in right pane
- Control Panel in Address bar drop-down list
- Switch to Classic view option shown in window's right pane
- Control Panel button depressed in taskbar

Other Ways

To activate items in an opened window or dialog box:
- Press Tab one or more times until you highlight the item and then press Enter.

Logging Off Windows XP

> **Tip:** Notice that there are other tabs available in Dialog boxes. Pressing those other tabs will reveal additional settings (more mouse property options in the example shown) that can be configured in Windows XP.

4. Click the **Mouse** icon to open the Mouse Properties dialog box with the Buttons tab displayed.

5. Slide (drag) the **Speed** adjustment slider in the middle of the Buttons tab to the right and test the new speed by double-clicking on the test folder in the preview area on the right.

6. Click the **Close** button to close the Mouse Properties dialog box without saving your changes. Then click the **Close** button in the Printers and Other Hardware window to return to the desktop.

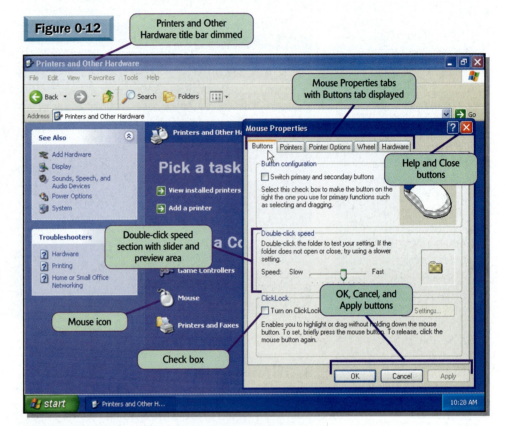

Figure 0-12

> **Other Ways:** To activate tabs in an opened window or dialog box:
> - Press Ctrl + Tab one or more times until the desired tab is displayed.

Logging Off Windows XP

After logging into your Windows XP workstation, you enter a secure environment where the operating system lets you accomplish tasks based on the rights assigned to you. When such conditions are no longer needed or you are done with your work session, you should log off Windows XP and leave the workstation ready for the next user.

Task 6:
To Log Off Windows XP

1 Display the Start menu, point to the **Log Off** button, and review the pop-up description for this button.

> **Tip** If you are working on a customized workstation that includes a workstation name (such as Computer Name), the Turn Off Computer button will appear as Turn Off *Computer Name*.

2 Click the **Log Off** button to open the Log Off Windows dialog box.

3 Point to the **Log Off** button in the dialog box and review the pop-up description.

4 Click the **Log Off** button to end the session and return to the Windows Welcome screen.

> **Tip** Another powerful effect showing the graphical nature of Windows XP is demonstrated as you begin log off procedures and the desktop background color slowly fades.

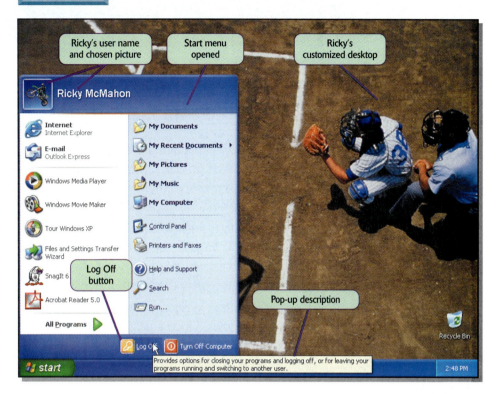

Figure 0-13

Figure 0-14

SUMMARY AND EXERCISES

SUMMARY

- The Windows XP Professional default configuration includes bright colors and modern graphics as part of the user interface, and it uses screen savers to preserve monitor resolution when there is no computer activity for extended periods.

- Windows XP starts automatically when you turn on the computer; you may have to log on to a network or select your user name and type a password to access the desktop. Some installations do not require users to log on, and the computer immediately displays the desktop.

- From the Windows Welcome screen, authorized users are permitted to log on to Windows. Once a password has been assigned, a user must enter it correctly each time, remembering that it is case sensitive. As passwords are typed in, their characters are represented by dots so others cannot read what is typed.

- Typical features found in Windows XP include the desktop, the Recycle Bin, the Start button, the taskbar, taskbar buttons, and a notification area.

- The mouse is an essential tool when working with the Windows XP graphical user interface, as is the desktop where the mouse is most frequently used.

- Mouse actions include such activities as pointing, pausing, clicking, dragging, right-clicking, double-clicking, and triple-clicking.

- Some objects offer pop-up descriptions when you pause the mouse pointer over them.

- Moving your mouse a small amount lets you find where the mouse pointer is located.

- Common window features include the title bar, panes, menu bar, toolbar, address bar, and the buttons available in the taskbar.

- Clicking the Start button opens the Start menu, which provides access to many features and applications. Small triangles on the right of many Start menu choices indicate additional cascading submenus that display even more choices.

- Start menu features include a user name and picture, the pinned area, separator lines, a recent applications area, cascade arrows, ellipsis items, and the Log Off and Turn Off Computer buttons.

- The ⊞ key can be used to display the Start menu.
- Common dialog box features include the title bar, the Help button, the Close button, text boxes, the OK button, the Cancel button, the Browse button, drop-down list boxes, option buttons, and check boxes.
- The mouse is likely the quickest way to perform tasks, but keystrokes are available for many tasks as well.
- Windows XP lets authorized users change common mouse features such as double-click speed through the Mouse Properties dialog box.
- In order to log off, the user should click the Log Off button in the Start menu. This activates the Log Off Windows dialog box, and dims the desktop.
- When leaving your workstation, you should log off the computer to end your session and return it to the log on point for the next user.

KEY TERMS & SKILLS

KEY TERMS

address bar (p. 13)
case sensitive (p. 4)
click (p. 6)
desktop (p. 2)
dialog boxes (p. 8)
double-click (p. 6)
drag (p. 6)
graphical user interface (GUI) (p. 5)
hovering (p. 6)
log on (p. 2)
menu bar (p. 13)
mouse (p. 5)
password (p. 2)
pause (p. 6)
point (p. 6)
pop-up description (p. 6)
Recycle Bin (p. 5)
right-click (p. 6)
screen saver (p. 3)
shortcut menu (p. 6)
Start button (p. 5)
Start menu (p. 8)
taskbar (p. 5)
title bar (p. 11)
toolbar (p. 13)
triple-click (p. 6)
user account (p. 2)
Windows Logo key (Winkey) (p. 9)
Windows Welcome screen (p. 3)

SKILLS

Boot the computer and log on Windows XP (p. 3)
Change mouse settings (p. 12)
Display and use the Start menu (p. 9)
Display cascading submenus (p. 10)
Log off Windows XP (p. 15)
Use the mouse on the desktop (p. 6)

STUDY QUESTIONS

MULTIPLE CHOICE

1. The small computer programs that run automatically to help preserve your monitor's resolution are called
   a. default device drivers.
   b. screen savers.
   c. Display Properties.
   d. third-party vendors.

2. Which of the following actions is usually used to activate a context-sensitive menu that applies to the intended object?
   a. right-click
   b. point
   c. double-click
   d. click

3. The GUI includes which of the following features?
   a. the desktop
   b. the Start button
   c. the taskbar
   d. all of the above.

4. Which of the following actions is usually used inside a text document to highlight a large block of text?
   a. point
   b. click
   c. triple-click
   d. double-click

5. If your user name has a password assigned, all of the following are displayed as components of the password entry box on your screen except
   a. the green arrow button.
   b. the blue question mark button.
   c. the white text box.
   d. the red X button.

6. The device that freed computer purists from having to laboriously key in all the commands needed by the computer to perform tasks was the
   a. monitor.
   b. GUI.
   c. mouse.
   d. keyboard.

7. Which of the following actions is usually used to highlight (or specify) an intended object or to place an insertion point in an intended location?
   a. drag
   b. click
   c. point
   d. double-click

8. Which of the following is an appropriate method for opening the Start menu?
   a. clicking the Start Menu button
   b. pressing the [W] key
   c. pressing the [Alt] key
   d. clicking the Start button

9. Using the Control Panel window as an example, which of the following is not an integral part of the window itself but can still be used to open or close the Control Panel window?
   a. the toolbar
   b. the menu bar
   c. the address bar
   d. the taskbar

10. Which of the following is commonly used to describe the action of holding your mouse pointer over a link or object for a few seconds to activate an informative message?
    a. cascading
    b. hovering
    c. hyperlinking
    d. clicking

SHORT ANSWER

1. What is a screen saver, and why do you use one?
2. What is found on the Windows Welcome screen?
3. Why should you be careful about someone behind you as you access your computer?
4. What is the purpose of the green arrow button when logging on using the Windows Welcome screen?
5. Describe the differences when using the ⊞ key instead of the mouse to navigate to an application through the Start menu.
6. Which mouse actions can be initiated by using the left mouse button?
7. When entering your password into the text box, what should you remember about the characters you enter?
8. What is the purpose of the area on the taskbar that is on the opposite end from the Start button?
9. What happens to the Recycle Bin if you double-click it as opposed to clicking it twice?
10. Why is it important to make sure you log off your computer when you are done working with Windows XP?

FILL IN THE BLANK

1. The _____ is an icon on the desktop that simulates the functions of a trash can and enables the user to discard objects that are not needed.
2. The _____, by default, is located at the left end of the taskbar.
3. You can use a(n) _____ button to bring an object into view or hide the object.

4. _____ over a link or object for a few seconds activates an informative message called a pop-up description (if one is associated with that link or object).
5. A mouse action that is used to execute a command, such as launching an application or opening a file is to _____.
6. Moving your _____ just a small amount lets you find where your mouse pointer is located.
7. Use the Tab key in a window or dialog box to _____ an object places a faintly visible box around that object.
8. You can slide the _____ in the middle of the Mouse Properties dialog box and test the new speed by double-clicking on the test folder on the right.
9. A(n) _____ identifies an item that displays additional menus that appear beside the active menu.
10. The _____ is used in a dialog box to request context-sensitive assistance from Windows XP.

FOR DISCUSSION

1. Explain the two methods for opening the Start menu and how they differ.
2. When would you be likely to encounter a screen saver?
3. Discuss two Windows XP security features explained in this project.
4. What is the significance of an ellipsis shown next to a menu item?
5. Explain the concept of cascading submenus.

PROJECT 1

Windows XP Professional Basics

Windows XP provides many customizable features to better suit your own needs or individual style. In this project, you will further explore the basics of Windows XP—the foundation you need to make working with Windows XP easier. In addition to changing your desktop's background, you will discover how to create folder objects, change folder options, and delete a folder from your desktop. You will also change your Recycle Bin configuration, work with options you can change on your own user account, and finally shut down your computer.

OBJECTIVES

After completing this project, you will be able to:

- Change the desktop background
- Create folder and file objects
- Work with folders
- Work with the Recycle Bin
- Change user options
- Switch users and shut down Windows XP

e-selections Running Case

So far, so good. Amber Wright is very pleased with your progress as her executive assistant in the e-Selections division of Selections, Inc. Your new position with your new computer that has Windows XP installed is working out well. Your quest to progress from answering the phones and sorting mail to performing more demanding functions that the company needs is proceeding nicely. You now continue expanding your basic knowledge of the new operating system by performing Windows XP tasks that Ms. Wright wants you to accomplish.

Windows XP Professional Basics

The Challenge

Ms. Wright wants to learn how the Recycle Bin's options can be changed, how to recover information accidentally deleted from the hard disk, how to customize folder options, and what user account settings can be customized without affecting administrator settings. Additionally, she wants to change her desktop graphic, switch users, and shut down her computer.

The Solution

Windows XP contains tools that will enable Ms. Wright to use a different desktop background, recover some of her deleted work, change the display of information in folders, work with folders, and switch users to allow someone else to use her computer.

Changing the Desktop Background

As you have already seen, Windows XP highlights its graphical nature by allowing you to customize your desktop. Using different background scenes enables you to personalize your desktop with a variety of graphics. Throughout this text series, different desktop backgrounds of various users will be used to further emphasize that capability.

In this project, you will notice a Windows XP graphic used as the desktop's background. In Project 0, Lauren used the *default configuration* (the initial installation settings) for the Windows XP desktop, while Ricky customized his with a baseball scene. Your desktop background may be as depicted in this task or possibly as specified by your instructor.

Troubleshooting Do not make any changes to your computer's display configurations unless you have permission.

Task 1:
To Change the Desktop Background

1 Display the Start menu, select **Control Panel** to open the Control Panel window, and click the **Appearance and Themes** category.

 Click the **Change the desktop background** button to open the Display Properties dialog box with the Desktop tab active.

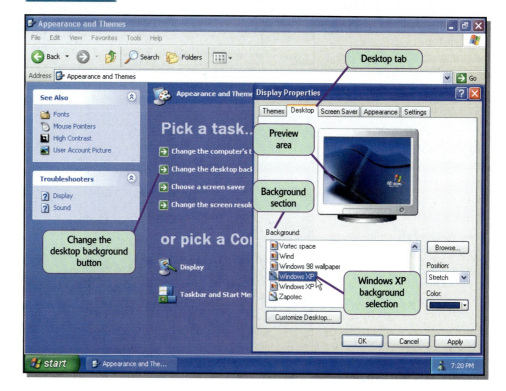

Figure 1-1

Other Ways
To open the Display Properties dialog box:
- Right-click a blank area of the desktop, select **Properties**, and click the tab for the dialog box page you want to view.

3 Scroll the **Background** list and select **Baseball wallpaper** to examine the baseball scene in the preview area of the Display Properties dialog box.

 4 Click the **Cancel** button to close the Display Properties dialog box without making any changes. Then click the **Close** button on the Appearance and Themes window to return to the desktop.

Figure 1-2

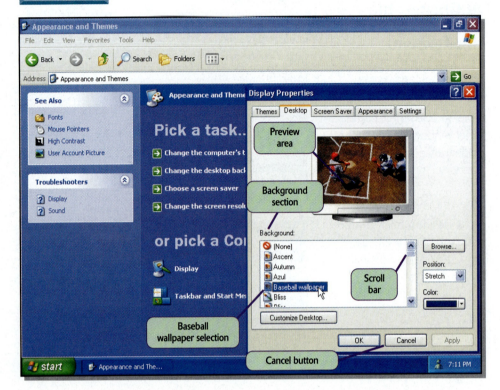

Troubleshooting If you have permission to change your desktop and you click the **OK** button at this point, you may see a Please Wait message box. Your screen will fade (as it does when you are changing users or logging off) before your new desktop background reappears.

Creating File and Folder Objects

One of the most common Windows XP tasks is creating new objects. *Objects* are entities with properties assigned (such as their names), and the most common objects are files and *folders*. Folders can be created to store other objects (including other folders) in order to organize information on the computer. In this task, you will create a new folder icon on the desktop and rename it.

 Tip Any object you can open and view on your computer screen can be classified as a *window* (which is where Windows got its name). A special type of window that can have other objects stored inside is a *folder*.

Task 2:
To Create File and Folder Objects

1 Right-click a blank area on the desktop to open the shortcut menu. Select **New** and then select **Folder**. A new folder appears on the desktop.

Figure 1-3

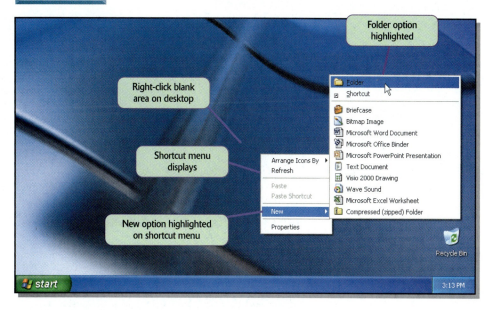

2 Type **Folder Settings** while the name is still highlighted.

> **Tip** When you create a new folder, the text *New Folder* is automatically highlighted. Typing new text when existing text is highlighted replaces highlighted text with the text you type.

Figure 1-4

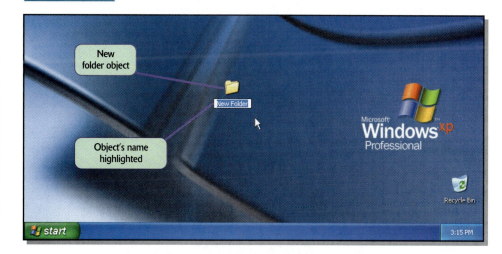

 Troubleshooting You should immediately begin typing the object's name after creating it. If you click anywhere else, the name will no longer be highlighted. If this happens, you can right-click the icon and select **Rename** from the shortcut menu to highlight the name once again so you can change it.

Creating File and Folder Objects

3 Press Enter to apply the folder name and exit the text entry mode.

Tip If you make a mistake while typing, you can use Bksp to go back one letter at a time or press Esc to cancel all text you entered.

Figure 1-5

4 Double-click the **Folder Settings** icon to display the Folder Settings window.

5 Right-click the blank area in the right pane to open the shortcut menu. Select **New** and then select **Text Document** to create a new text file inside the new folder.

Tip Notice that the file name for the new text document is highlighted, similar to when you created a New Folder.

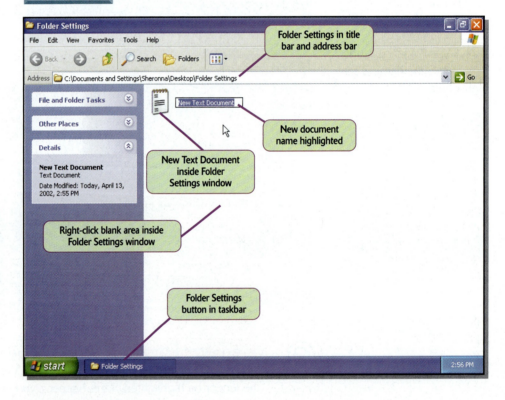

Figure 1-6

Windows XP Professional Basics

WN 1-7

6 Type **Test Document** while the name is still highlighted.

7 Press Enter to apply the document name. Then click the **Close** button to close the Folder Settings window and return to the desktop.

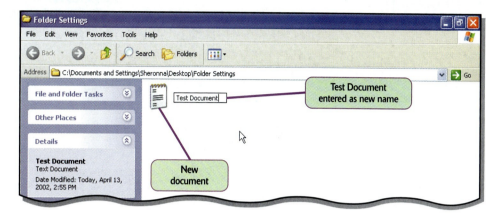

Figure 1-7

Working with Folders

Another setting you can alter when customizing your own environment deals with the way folders are displayed on your screen, how objects inside folders are used, and whether other folders can be viewed at all. Changing folder options allows you to customize how you organize or find the objects you frequently use.

CHECK POINT

Remember those ellipses appearing with menu items that required additional entries? This task uses a command with an ellipsis on the Tools drop-down menu. The resulting dialog box enables you to supply information on several tabbed windows.

Troubleshooting Default settings may have been changed by your administrator (or another user) prior to your performing this task, and your settings (and views) may not be the same as indicated. If so, you can still perform this exercise but do not alter any settings without permission.

Task 3:
To Work with Folders

1 Double-click the **Folder Settings** icon created in Task 2 to open the folder.

2 Click **Tools** in the menu bar and select **Folder Options**. The Folder Options dialog box appears.

To open the Folder Settings folder:
- Click the folder icon to highlight it and press Enter.

To open the Folder Options dialog box from the Folder Settings window:
- Press Alt + T + O.

Figure 1-8

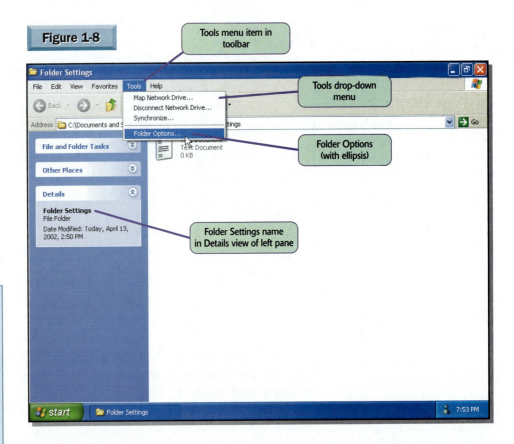

- Tools menu item in toolbar
- Tools drop-down menu
- Folder Options (with ellipsis)
- Folder Settings name in Details view of left pane

Tip: When using the Alt key to choose menu commands, the menu items display an underlined letter. These letters, sometimes referred to as *hotkeys,* can be used to invoke the menu items by simply pressing the underlined letter on the keyboard.

Windows XP Professional Basics WN 1-9

3 Click the **Open each folder in its own window** option button. Then click the **Cancel** button to return to the Folder Settings window without making any changes.

4 Click the **Close** button in the Folder Settings window. The Folder Settings window closes, and you are returned to the desktop.

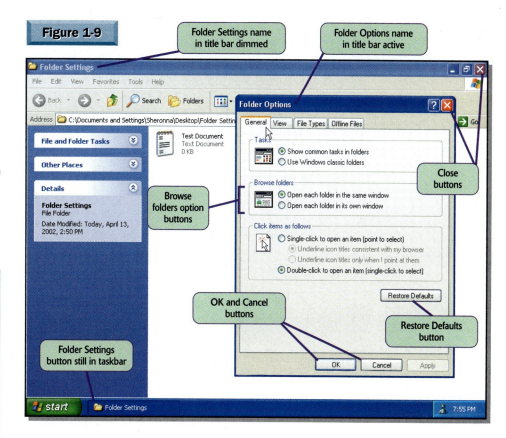

Figure 1-9

> **Tip**
>
> Clicking the **OK** button in a dialog box applies all the changes you have selected. Clicking the **Cancel** button or the **Close** button ignores any changes you made that have not been applied. Clicking the **Restore Defaults** button resets the configuration on a dialog box to the default (original) settings.

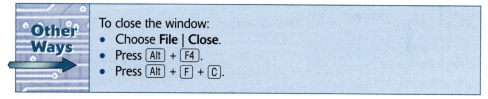

Other Ways

To close the window:
- Choose **File | Close**.
- Press `Alt` + `F4`.
- Press `Alt` + `F` + `C`.

CHECK POINT

Whether you choose to open folders in their own window or have each consecutive window open in the same space will be a preference you should determine after much computer use. Having separate windows can become confusing, but not having the windows you need open can be unproductive as well.

Using the Recycle Bin

As you learned previously, the Recycle Bin stores items that you delete, such as document files, graphics, folders, and so on. You can retrieve items from the Recycle Bin and restore them to their original location until you empty the Recycle Bin and permanently delete these items. Windows XP enables you to change certain Recycle Bin settings to suit your own needs.

Changing Recycle Bin Settings

The Recycle Bin, by default, sits in the lower right corner of your desktop after you install Windows XP. The default settings may include one setting that designates the use of the Recycle Bin and another that requires confirmation, but both these settings can be changed. Additionally, even though the Recycle Bin's default maximum storage size is 10% of the computer's local *hard disk drive* space (your computer's internal storage device), it can also be changed to suit your own needs.

Microsoft calls the Recycle Bin a "safety net when deleting files and folders" because it acts as a temporary storage area for discarded items prior to their permanent erasure from your hard drive. When you delete an object or drag it to the Recycle Bin, by default Windows XP will ask for confirmation and then store these items until you need them back (or you permanently erase them).

CHECK POINT

Remember that a dialog box is a special type of window with buttons or other items for setting system or application options. Most dialog boxes have multiple tabs that are used for setting different configurations. Use the **Apply** button to invoke the settings as you make them, while keeping the dialog box open, so you can check or change other settings as well.

Task 4:
To Change Recycle Bin Settings

1 Right-click the **Recycle Bin** icon to display the shortcut menu and select **Properties**. The Recycle Bin Properties dialog box appears.

Figure 1-10

Troubleshooting

The Recycle Bin's storage is used only for items discarded from the hard drive on your own computer (the *local machine*). Any files or folders deleted from other areas (floppy disk, zip disk, or network disk) or too large to fit in the Recycle Bin's maximum size constraint are immediately erased and cannot be recovered.

Windows XP Professional Basics

2 Select the **Do not move files to the Recycle Bin** check box and clear the check mark from the **Display delete confirmation dialog** check box.

3 Select the **Configure drives independently** option button and click the **Local Disk (C:)** tab to see the local disk's Recycle Bin size settings.

> **Tip** If you select the **Do not move files to the Recycle Bin** check box, Windows XP permanently erases objects you delete instead of storing them in the Recycle Bin.

Figure 1-11

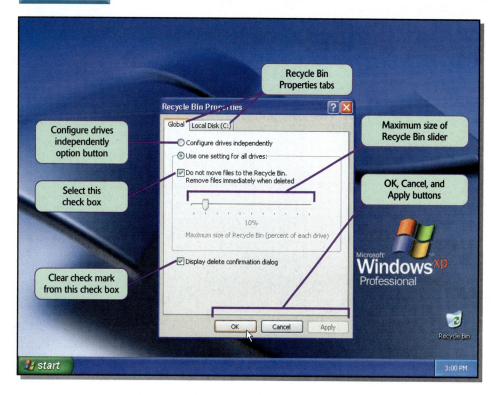

> **Tip** Clearing the check mark from the **Display delete confirmation dialog** check box tells Windows XP to immediately discard anything you delete, without displaying a confirmation. Normally, when you press [Delete], you must confirm the deletion. Any deleted item that is larger than the Recycle Bin's maximum storage capacity is immediately erased and cannot be recovered.

Using the Recycle Bin

4 Slide the **Maximum size of Recycle Bin** slider to set its size at **2%** of your local drive.

 Note that the space reserved for the Recycle Bin changes as the slider moves.

5 Click the **Cancel** button to close the dialog box and return to the desktop without invoking any of the changes you have made.

Figure 1-12

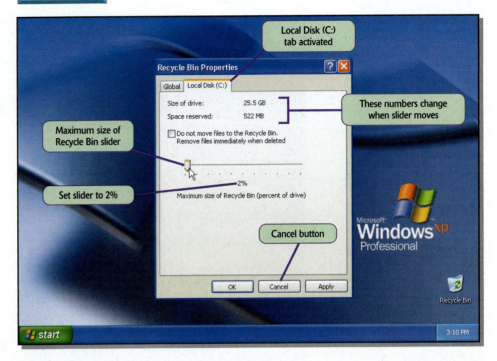

Deleting and Restoring Recycle Bin Items

Once you have created an object, you should also know how to get rid of it. Windows XP places a lot of emphasis on keeping the desktop clean and deleting extraneous objects (such as the empty folder created in Task 2). Deleting files or folders you no longer need helps keep your desktop in order.

 Troubleshooting You should note whether or not the Recycle Bin indicates items are already stored inside. If it does, the icon will show papers inside the trash bin, and you will have to empty its contents in order to see the effect of deleting more items. You should request instructor permission prior to deleting these items.

Task 5:
To Delete and Restore Recycle Bin Items

1 Right-click the **Folder Settings** icon to open a shortcut menu and select **Delete**. The Confirm Folder Delete dialog box appears.

Figure 1-13

Other Ways

To delete the Folder Settings icon from your desktop:
- Drag the Folder Settings icon and drop it on the Recycle Bin icon.
- Click the Folder Settings icon and press Delete.

2 Click the **Yes** button in the Confirm Folder Delete dialog box to delete the folder.

Tip If your default Recycle Bin settings have not been altered, this deletes your new Folder Settings folder from your desktop and puts it in the Recycle Bin. If the settings have been changed, you may not get a confirmation when you delete the folder from your desktop, and you will not be able to restore the folder back to the desktop.

Figure 1-14

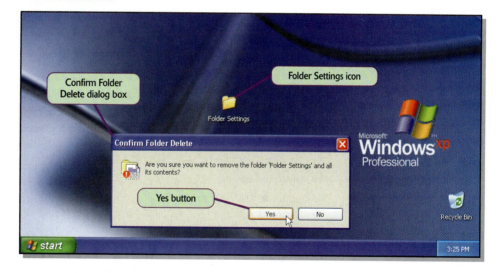

3 Double-click the **Recycle Bin** icon to open the Recycle Bin. Right-click the **Folder Settings** icon, select **Restore** to return the deleted folder to the desktop, and click the **Close** button to close the Recycle Bin.

4 Click the **Folder Settings** icon, press Delete, and click the **Yes** button to delete the folder again.

5 Right-click the **Recycle Bin** icon, click **Empty Recycle Bin**, click the **Yes** button in the Confirm File Delete dialog box to permanently delete the file from the Recycle Bin.

Figure 1-15

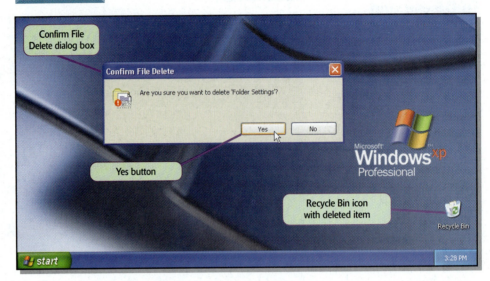

 Tip Once you place discarded items in the Recycle Bin, you may decide to leave them there for awhile as an added measure of security—just in case you later need what you temporarily thought was trash. However, be aware that another user may empty the Recycle Bin at a later time.

Changing User Options

You have already seen several settings and numerous options that can be set to customize your working environment. Windows XP also enables you to alter the way your user name is represented on your computer.

 CHECK POINT

You will notice that the desktop in this task uses Lauren's settings. Recall from Project 0 that a user account gains you access to Windows XP. There are two local user account types on a Windows XP workstation—a *computer administrator account* and a *limited account*. Lauren's user account is a limited account, so she is restricted to changing user settings for only a few items. A computer administrator account can make more changes, and those changes can involve any user account.

 Troubleshooting Default settings may have been changed by your administrator (or another user) prior to your performing this task, and your settings may not be the same as indicated. If so, you can still perform this exercise but do not alter any settings without permission.

Task 6:
To Change User Options

1 Display the Start menu and pause over **Control Panel** to read its pop-up description.

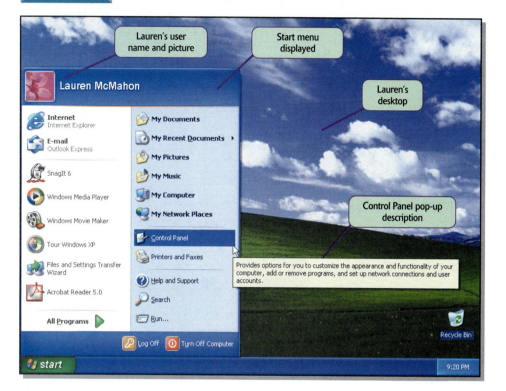

Figure 1-16

2 Select **Control Panel** to open the Control Panel.

> **Tip** Notice that the title bar has the name Control Panel and the taskbar contains a Control Panel button that appears depressed, showing that the folder is actively being used. These are both indications that the Control Panel is the *active window*.

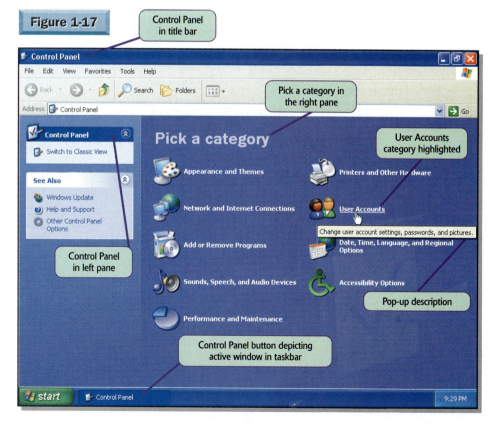

Figure 1-17

Changing User Options

3 Click the **User Accounts** category in the right pane to open that folder's **Pick a task** section and view the tasks that you can alter.

> **Tip** Notice how few items can be changed when your user account does not have *administrative privileges* (those necessary to control access and use). Administrators control and maintain systems such as your computer. Your account is most likely a limited account.

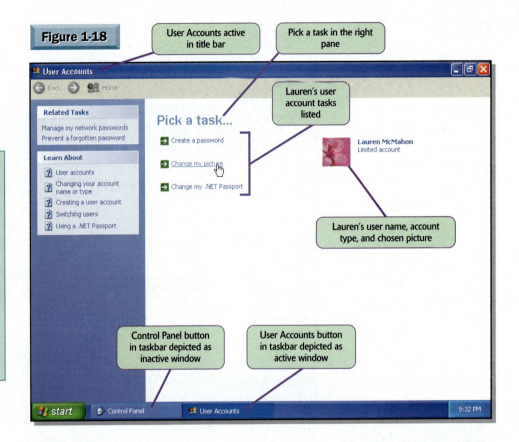

Figure 1-18

- User Accounts active in title bar
- Pick a task in the right pane
- Lauren's user account tasks listed
- Lauren's user name, account type, and chosen picture
- Control Panel button in taskbar depicted as inactive window
- User Accounts button in taskbar depicted as active window

> **Tip** Notice that the title bar now has the name User Accounts, and the taskbar contains a User Accounts button that is depressed (the active window) as well as a Control Panel button that is not depressed (an *inactive window*).

4 Click the **Change my picture** button and click a new picture of your choice from those presented in the **Pick a new picture for your account** section. Notice that the picture you choose and the **Change Picture** button are both highlighted.

> **Tip** You can drag the scroll bar along the right side of the displayed pictures and view the alternative pictures available. This action is called *scrolling* and is a method for advancing the window up or down to display hidden information. Notice that the **Back** button is highlighted and ready to use as a method of returning to the previous window before applying any changes.

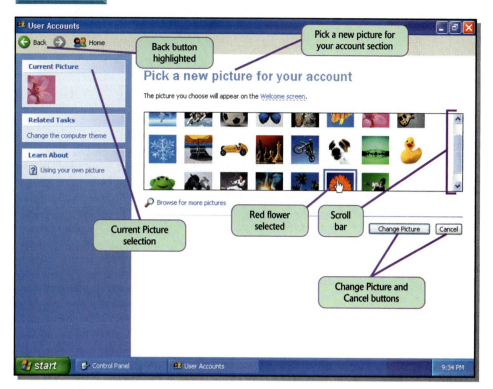

Figure 1-19

5 Click the **Change Picture** button if you have permission to make changes; otherwise click the **Cancel** button.

6 Click the **Close** button to close the User Accounts window. Then click the **Close** button again to close the Control Panel window.

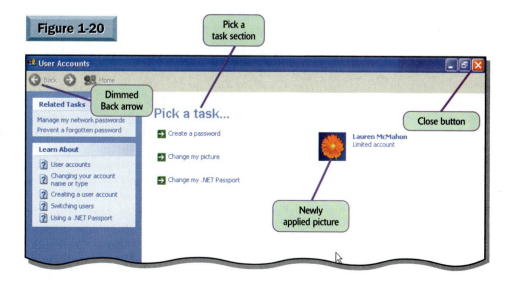

Figure 1-20

> **Tip** If you have permission and make the change, notice that the **Back** button is no longer highlighted for use. Once you apply the change, you can no longer go back to the previous page. You have to manually change your picture back to the former picture.

Switching Users and Shutting Down Windows XP

Windows XP offers two options for leaving the computer after completing your work. These options include (1) logging off and leaving the computer running so that another user can log on and (2) shutting down the computer when it will remain unused for an extended period of time. To ensure that all files are stored properly, it is important to perform a proper *shut down* to turn off the computer. When you perform a shut-down procedure, Windows XP presents the alternatives described in Table 1-1.

Table 1-1	Windows XP Shut Down Options
Option	**Description**
Log off	Ends your current session and returns the still-running computer to the Windows Welcome screen, ready for the next authorized user to log on and use the computer.
Switch User	Keeps your current session (and all your current activities) running and returns the still-running computer to the Windows Welcome screen, ready for the next authorized user to log on and use the computer.
Hibernate (or Stand By)	Shuts down the computer after storing your current session (and all your current activities) on your hard disk such that you can quickly restore your session to where you were prior to hibernating.
Shut Down (or Turn Off Computer)	Ends your current session (and all other users' current sessions) by allowing Windows XP to close all open files, store all of its operating system commands, and discard any temporary working items it has been using.
Restart	Performs a shut down and then immediately initiates the start-up procedures without turning the computer off.

CHECK POINT

You will notice here that the procedures for shutting down are basically the same when Ricky first changes users (via the **Switch User** button) and then shuts the computer down in the process of restarting it. Performing a shut down allows Windows XP to go through the required closing procedures and properly store all of the operating system commands needed for its next session.

Troubleshooting Do not click the **Hibernate** button (or **Stand By** button if you have a laptop computer), the **Turn Off** button, or the **Restart** button on your computer unless you have permission. Doing so may terminate any work currently in progress by other properly logged on users.

Task 7:
To Switch Users and Shut Down Windows XP

1 Display the Start menu and click the **Log Off** button to display the Log Off Windows dialog box. Point to the **Switch User** button and read the last note at the bottom of the pop-up description.

Troubleshooting
If you or your administrator has customized your workstation and assigned a name to the computer, your **Shut Down Computer** button (or **Turn off computer** button) will insert that customized name in place of "Computer."

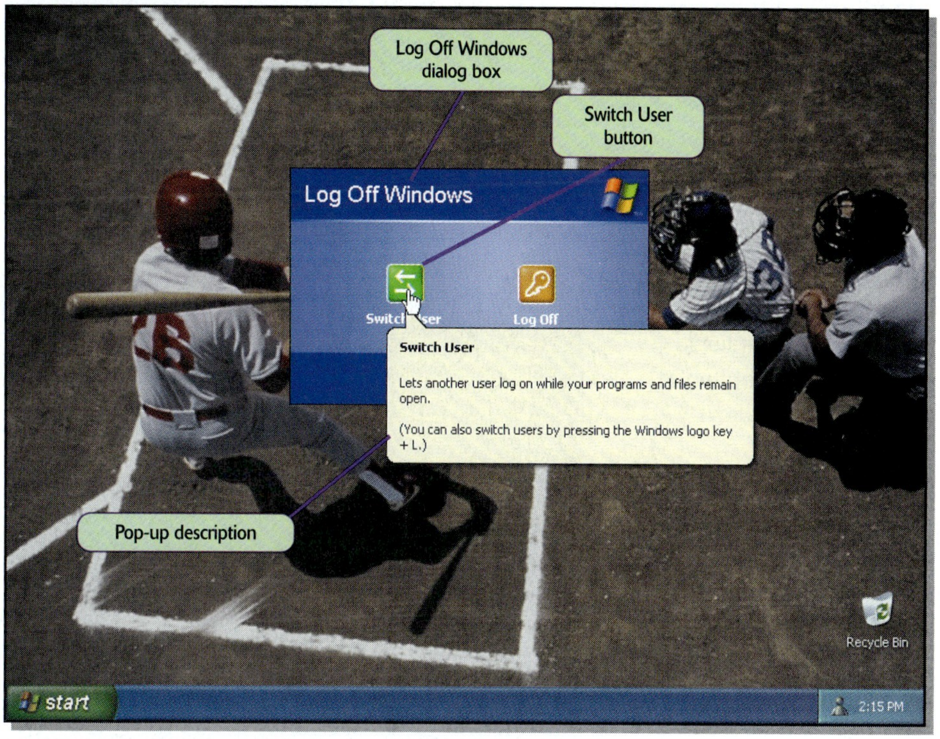

2 Click the **Switch User** button to go to the Windows Welcome screen and then click the **Turn off computer** (or Turn Off *customized name*) button. The Turn off computer dialog box displays.

Troubleshooting
Having too many users working active applications on the computer through use of the Switch User function can degrade the workstation's operational capabilities.

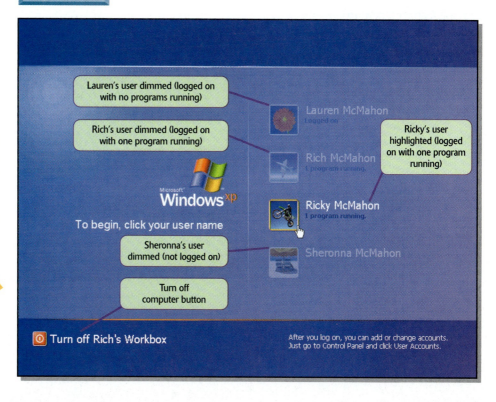

Figure 1-21

Figure 1-22

Switching Users and Shutting Down Windows XP

Tip: The Switch User option leaves your current applications or opened objects in their current state while you allow another authorized user to log on to the workstation. It then immediately returns you to the same state when that second user finishes and you log back on to the computer.

3 Point to the **Hibernate**, **Turn Off**, and **Restart** buttons to note their features in their respective pop-up descriptions. Click the **Cancel** button to return to the Windows Welcome Screen.

4 Click the picture for your user name and enter your password, if necessary, to return to your desktop.

5 Display the Start menu and click the **Turn off computer** button. Depending on your permissions, click **Hibernate**, **Turn Off**, or **Restart** to turn the computer off; you can also click the **Cancel** button to return to the Windows Welcome screen so you can log off.

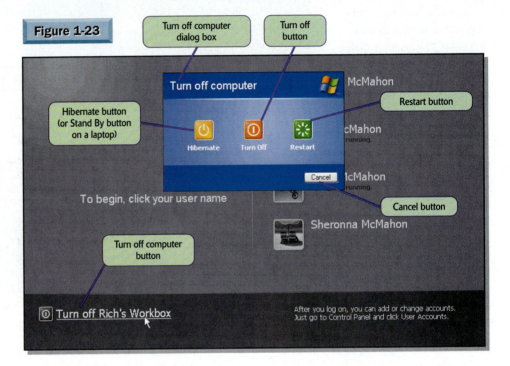

Figure 1-23

SUMMARY AND EXERCISES

SUMMARY

- The Recycle Bin settings can be changed to further customize your environment.
- Folders are created to store other objects (including other folders) to organize information on the computer.
- When you create a folder, its name is already highlighted to facilitate an immediate name change.
- The ellipsis used with the Start menu and menu bar items indicates that a dialog box, sometimes with several tabs, will be displayed when you select the command.
- You can press [Alt] for a menu navigation technique that involves pressing underlined letters, or hotkeys, instead of clicking menu items with your mouse.
- You can set your folders so each opens in its own window instead of the default option, where they open in the same window.
- Pausing your mouse pointer over most buttons reveals a pop-up description that gives the button's purpose.
- If you delete an object, the Recycle Bin has a setting that allows your item to stay there until the Recycle Bin is emptied manually.
- There are two local user account types—computer administrator accounts and limited accounts.
- Limited account users may be able to change the picture icon displayed at the top of their Start menu.
- The Windows Welcome screen lists individuals who are granted access, indicates who is currently logged on to the computer, and shows whether or not users have programs running.
- The Switch User option allows a second user (or more) to log on to the computer without requiring other logged-on users to end their session. The previous users' sessions are kept running in the background.
- In order to switch users, the user must click the Log Off button in the Start menu. This activates the Log Off Windows dialog box, and the desktop is dimmed to highlight the log off options that are available.
- Use the Display Properties dialog box to change the desktop wallpaper displayed as your desktop background.
- In order to shut down the computer, the user must click the Turn off computer (or Turn off *customized name*) button in the Start menu. This activates the Turn Off Windows dialog box, and the desktop is dimmed to highlight the shut down options that are available.

KEY TERMS & SKILLS

KEY TERMS

active window (p. 1-15)
administrative privileges (p. 1-16)
computer administrator account (p. 1-14)
default configuration (p. 1-2)
folder (p. 1-4)
hard disk drive (p. 1-10)
hibernate (p. 1-18)
hotkeys (p. 1-8)
inactive window (p. 1-16)
limited account (p. 1-14)
local machine (p. 1-10)
log off (p. 1-18)
objects (p. 1-4)
restart (p. 1-18)
scrolling (p. 1-17)
shut down (p. 1-18)
window (p. 1-4)

SKILLS

Change the desktop background (p. 1-3)
Change Recycle Bin options (p. 1-10)
Change user options (p. 1-15)
Create folder and file objects (p. 1-5)
Delete and restore Recycle Bin items (p. 1-13)
Switch users and shut down Windows XP (p. 1-19)
Work with folders (p. 1-8)

STUDY QUESTIONS

MULTIPLE CHOICE

1. What default Recycle Bin setting requires you to confirm every file or folder deletion?
   a. the maximum size of Recycle Bin slider
   b. the Help button
   c. the Delete Confirmation button
   d. a check box

2. What is the default maximum size setting for the Recycle Bin?
   a. 10%
   b. 20%
   c. 10 megabytes
   d. 20 megabytes

3. When working with dialog boxes, which button typically is used, if available, when you want to implement changed settings but keep the dialog box open?
   a. OK
   b. Cancel
   c. Apply
   d. Close

4. Which of the following is used to store other objects to organize information on your computer?
   a. file
   b. folder
   c. Recycle Bin
   d. window

5. Which of the following is highlighted when you first create a new folder?
   a. the Recycle Bin
   b. the icon picture
   c. the folder name
   d. the icon

6. If you make a mistake while typing a folder name, which of the following is used to go back one character at a time?
   a. [Delete]
   b. [Alt]
   c. [Bksp]
   d. [Esc]

7. Which of the following is the name of the underlined letter onscreen when using the optional [Alt] key menu navigation technique?
   a. Shiftkeys
   b. StickyKeys
   c. ClickKeys
   d. Hotkeys

8. Which of the following is one of two types of local users on a Windows XP Professional computer?
   a. network administrator
   b. domain user
   c. limited account
   d. computer user

9. Which of the following is *not* a method that can be used to close a folder's window?
   a. Choose File | Close.
   b. Double-click the folder's title bar.
   c. Press [Alt] + [F] + [C].
   d. Press [Alt] + [F4].

10. Which of the following options does not facilitate Windows XP going through its procedure of shutting down all its open files and discarding any temporary working items it has been using?
    a. Switch User
    b. Hibernate
    c. Shut Down
    d. Restart

SHORT ANSWER

1. After a default installation of Windows XP workstation, which item sits in the lower right corner of your desktop and allows a maximum size limitation to be imposed in its configuration settings?
2. What opens when you right-click on the Recycle Bin?
3. What happens when you first create a new folder on the desktop?
4. Which menu bar item contains the entry used to activate the Folder Options dialog box?
5. If a folder is already highlighted, what is the easiest way to open it?
6. Which key on the keyboard is usually pressed to initiate the use of hotkeys?
7. What are the two browse folder options available on Windows XP?
8. How can you tell, without opening it, if there is trash in the Recycle Bin?
9. What is the indication in the taskbar that shows which window is active?
10. What are the two types of local user accounts on a Windows XP computer?

FILL IN THE BLANK

1. A(n) _____ appears when you right-click on an object.
2. Clearing the _____ check box tells the system to immediately discard anything you delete.
3. You can use the _____ tab to see your computer's Recycle Bin size settings.
4. Most dialog boxes have multiple _____ that are used for different setting configurations.

5. Clicking a dialog box's _____ button closes it and returns to your previous location without making any of the changes you have made.
6. If you make an error when typing an object's name and wish to start over, press the _____ key.
7. The _____ on the right side of the Folder Options command in the Tools drop-down menu indicates that it has an associated dialog box.
8. The use of _____ involves using underlined letters to invoke menu items.
9. The _____ folder options setting configures your folders to use only one window.
10. Right-clicking the title bar and pressing the letter _____ closes the applicable window.

FOR DISCUSSION

1. Explain the two browse folder options and how they differ.
2. When would you have to create a computer administrator account for a user instead of a limited account?
3. Discuss the Recycle Bin's maximum size restriction.
4. Why is it important to properly shut down a Windows XP workstation?
5. Explain the concept of hibernation that is available in a Windows XP Professional installation but not part of a server-based network.

GUIDED EXERCISES

1 CHANGING RECYCLE BIN SETTINGS

Your department head authorized you to change the maximum size of your Recycle Bin to twice its default size. Some of the files you thought would be there for later restoration were not stored in the Recycle Bin, so you need to change these settings as well.

1. Right-click the **Recycle Bin** icon and select **Properties**.
2. Click the **Global** tab and select the **Use one setting for all drives** option button.
3. Clear the check mark from the **Do not move files to the Recycle Bin** check box.
4. Slide the **Maximum size of Recycle Bin** slider to set its size at 20%.
5. Click the **Cancel** button to close the dialog box and return to the desktop without invoking any of the changes you have made.

2 RESTORING DEFAULT FOLDER OPTIONS

You have been instructed to restore the default folder options on all the computers in your department. In the past, users have been allowed to change these settings on their own, and you are making this change to standardize how folder options are set. Follow these steps to restore the folder options.

1. Right-click a blank spot on your desktop, select New, and select Folder, and then enter Folder Settings as your new folder's name.
2. Double-click the **Folder Settings** folder.
3. Click **Tools | Folder Options** in the menu bar.
4. Click the **General** tab of the Folder Options dialog box.
5. Click the **Restore Defaults** button.
6. Click the **OK** button to apply the change and close the Folder Options dialog box if you actually have permission to change your computer settings; otherwise, click the **Cancel** button to disregard your changes.
7. Click the **Close** button on the Folder Settings window to return to the desktop.

3 CHANGING YOUR USER ACCOUNT PICTURE

You obtained permission to change the picture associated with your user account. Follow these steps to change your user account picture.

1. Click the **Start** button and select **Control Panel**.
2. Click the **User Accounts** category.
3. Click the **Change my picture** button.
4. Scroll through the window and double-click your new picture.
5. Click the **Close** button two times to close the open windows.

ON YOUR OWN

The difficulty of these case studies varies: ▶ are the least difficult; ▶▶ are more difficult; and ▶▶▶ are the most difficult.

1 CREATING NEW FILE AND FOLDER OBJECTS

▶ Create a new folder on the desktop named **File Types**. Open the folder and create new objects for each of the object types available when you select **New** from a shortcut menu in the File Types window. As a minimum, you should create three objects, named My Folder, My Bitmap, and My Text Document.

2 DELETING FILE TYPES

▶ Open the File Types folder you created in On Your Own exercise 1 and delete the individual files you created inside that folder. After deleting all your new files, use the Recycle Bin to restore each file back to the File Types folder. Then delete the File Types folder with its contents and empty the Recycle Bin.

3 EMBEDDING FOLDERS

▶▶ Create a new folder on your desktop named **Embedded Folders**. Open that folder and create another new folder named **Embedded One**. Open that folder and create another new folder named **Embedded Two**. Continue creating new embedded folders and naming them one at a time until you have created up through **Embedded Ten**. Open that tenth folder and create a new text document inside named **Finally**. Close all open items, drag your Embedded Folders icon to the Recycle Bin, and then empty the Recycle Bin to erase your embedded folders.

4 PREVIEWING DESKTOP BACKGROUNDS

 Preview each of the following desktop backgrounds on the Desktop tab of the Display Properties dialog box. Click Cancel when you are done.

- Ascent
- Dangerous Creatures wallpaper
- Friend
- Home
- Inside Your Computer wallpaper
- Jungle wallpaper
- Leonardo da Vinci wallpaper
- Mystery wallpaper
- Nature wallpaper
- Radiance
- Science wallpaper
- Space wallpaper
- Sports wallpaper
- Stonehenge
- The 60's USA wallpaper
- The Golden Era wallpaper
- Travel wallpaper
- Underwater wallpaper

5 USING THE HIBERNATE OPTION WITH A FOLDER OPEN

Create a new folder on your desktop named **Still Open** and open that folder. Log off and go to the Windows Welcome screen using the Switch User button to verify your user's status. Log back on and verify that your folder is still open. Turn off the computer using the Hibernate button. Restart and verify that your folder is still open. Close the Still Open folder, delete it, and empty the Recycle Bin to erase it.

PROJECT 2

Working with Files and Folders

In this project, you will learn more about working with the file and folder tools introduced in Project 1. You will learn to navigate Windows XP Professional, use the computer's user interface, and alter some of the operating system settings and options. Finally, you will learn to manipulate, delete, and restore files and folders; where to gather hard drive details; how to conduct a basic search; and how to format a floppy disk.

OBJECTIVES

After completing this project, you will be able to:

- Use files and folders
- Work with windows
- Switch between My Computer and Windows Explorer views
- Navigate in Windows Explorer
- Customize the Start menu
- Gather hard drive details
- Conduct a basic search
- Format a floppy disk

e-selections Running Case

As the executive assistant in the e-Selections division of Selections, Inc., you have now started performing the higher-level administrative functions you set out to learn. Your plan to instruct Ms. Wright has been proceeding smoothly as well. Now you need to learn the basics of working with files and folders so you can share this knowledge with Ms. Wright.

PROJECT 2

Working with Files and Folders

The Challenge

Amber Wright is delighted with your progress as both her executive assistant and tutor. She has some specific needs and wants you to help her accomplish the following:

- Become more proficient working with her files and folders
- Explain how she can better use the My Documents folder
- Demonstrate different ways to navigate through her computer with Windows Explorer
- Become more proficient in using her desktop
- Adjust her Start menu to show a different picture than initially installed
- Collect the details needed to make decisions about her computer storage
- Conduct basic searches
- Create a formatted floppy disk

The Solution

Since you will be working with many files and folders, such as the My Documents folder, you need to be as proficient with them as possible. You will work with Windows XP until you develop a thorough understanding of navigating through your computer with Windows Explorer. You will also become very comfortable working in Windows XP's desktop environment, changing the Start menu, and altering user configurations. Additionally, you will acquire the information needed to show others how to collect storage information, conduct extensive searches, and format floppy disks.

Using Files and Folders

Because files and folders are the items that you will most often work with, you should become very comfortable with their use. Working with them often and understanding their many features will help you become proficient when opening, closing, resizing, moving, copying, deleting, and restoring these objects. In the next few tasks, these actions will be demonstrated.

Working with Files and Folders   WN 2-3

Using File and Folder Tools

In order to effectively use the file and folder skills you developed in Project 1, you must become more proficient with the tools available to you. Many of these tools are available to you in each window you display in Windows XP. Other tools help you organize and keep your workspace free of clutter. The most commonly used of the file and folder tools are the three buttons on the right side of each window's title bar: *Minimize, Maximize/Restore Down*, and *Close* buttons, respectively. Additionally, each window includes resizing arrows so you can customize your viewing space. In this task, you will learn to use the tools available to you when working with files and folders.

Task 1:
To Use File and Folder Tools

1 Choose **Start | My Documents** to open the My Documents window.

> **Troubleshooting**
> Your desktop may appear differently than the figures displayed in this and the following tasks because some of your computer's default settings have likely been changed. Such changes should have little effect on any of these lessons.

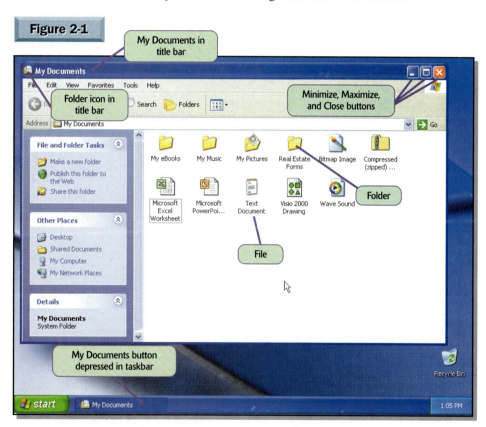

Figure 2-1

2 Click the **Minimize** button. The My Documents window is no longer visible on the desktop.

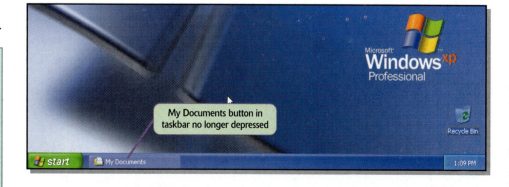

Figure 2-2

> **Tip** Notice that the My Documents button in the taskbar is no longer depressed because the My Documents folder is no longer the active window. Using the Minimize button helps reduce clutter on the desktop.

3 Click the **My Documents** button in the taskbar. The My Documents window opens to the same size it was before you clicked the Minimize button.

4 Click the **Maximize** button, if the window does not already fill the screen. The button changes to the Restore Down button.

5 Click the **Restore Down** button to restore the window to its former size. The button changes back to the Maximize button.

Figure 2-3

Tip — Although the button's full name is the Maximize/Restore Down button, it is most commonly referred to simply as the Maximize button or the Restore button, depending on its current state. In this case, you are restoring it to its former size so it would be called the Restore button.

Other Ways — To access Minimize, Maximize, Restore, or Close:
- Click the Control menu icon (on the far left of the title bar) to reveal the Control menu and then select the desired function.

6 Point to the right edge of the My Documents window to show the double-headed horizontal arrow; then drag the arrow to the left to shrink the window.

Figure 2-4

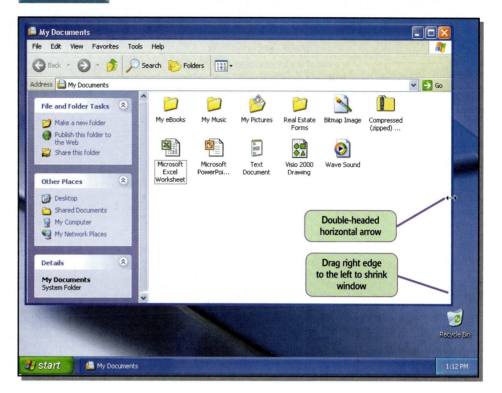

7 Point to the bottom edge of the My Documents window to show the double-headed vertical arrow; then drag the arrow up to shrink the window.

Figure 2-5

8 Point to the lower right corner of the My Documents window to show the double-headed diagonal arrow; then drag the arrow up and to the left to shrink the window.

9 Double-click the Control Menu icon at the left end of the title bar to close the My Documents window.

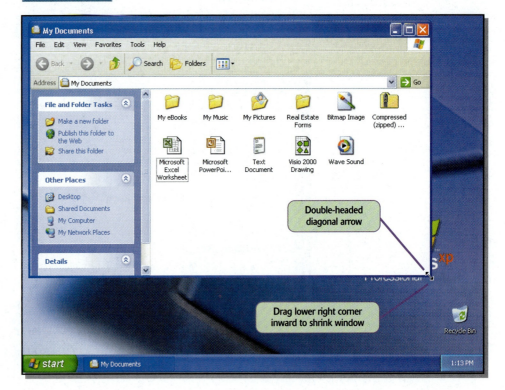

Figure 2-6

Changing Folder Views in My Documents

When you are working with folders, you may want to use different views to see the objects stored within them. The *Views button* offers a context sensitive list of different views available for showing these objects. You should become familiar with the different ways of depicting the items so you can customize your computer to fit your own desires.

Task 2:
To Change Folder Views in My Documents

1 Choose **Start | My Documents** to open the My Documents window and maximize the window if it is not already full size on your screen.

2 Click the **Views** button in the toolbar and select **Icons**. Notice the Icons view of the objects displayed in the window.

Figure 2-7

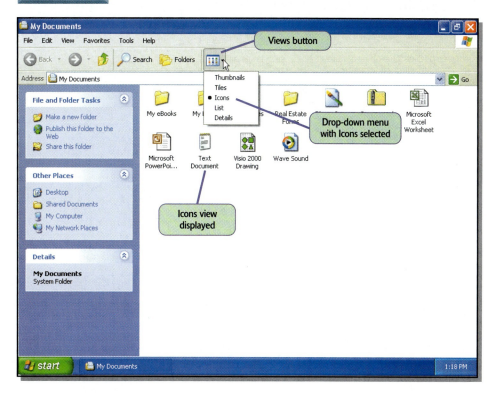

3 Click the **Views** button in the toolbar and select **Tiles**. Notice the Tiles view of the objects displayed in the window.

Figure 2-8

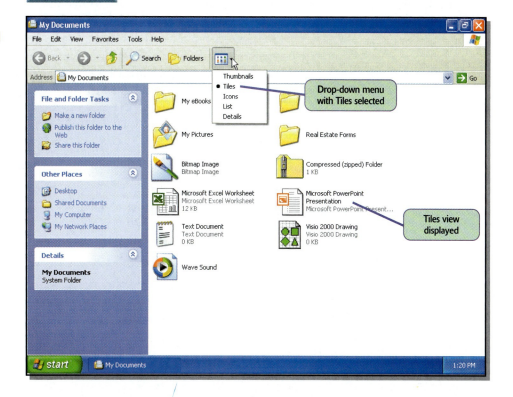

4 Click the **Views** button in the toolbar and select **Thumbnails**. Notice the Thumbnails view of the objects displayed in the window.

5 Continue this sampling process for each of the remaining views (List and Details) available by using the Views button and return to the Icons view when finished.

> **Tip** The icons displayed in these views are determined by a three-digit code added to the object's name when it is created, such as "txt" for a text file and "doc" for a Microsoft Word file. Depending on your computer's configuration, these digits may be visible or hidden as in the examples shown.

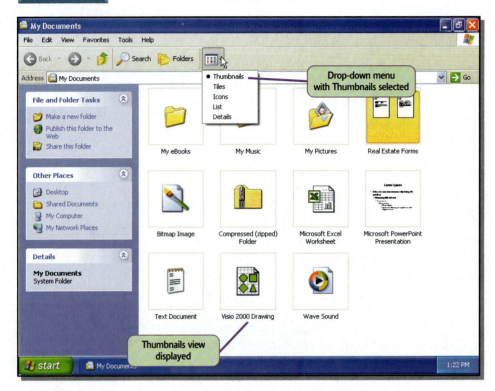

Figure 2-9

Manipulating Files and Folders

Now that you are familiar with files and folders, you should become more proficient working with them. At various times, you will have to copy or move files and folders to various locations or even rename them. In this task, you will learn to make these changes as well as to delete and then restore a file.

Task 3:
To Manipulate Files and Folders

1 Choose **Start | My Documents** to open the My Documents folder. Click **Make a new folder** in the File and Folder Tasks section of the left pane, type the name **Working Materials**, and press Enter.

2 Double-click the **Working Materials** folder to open it in the same window and resize the window as shown in the example. Choose **File | New | Text Document**, type the name **Working Text**, and press Enter.

3 Pause the mouse pointer over the **Working Text** file, press and hold down the right mouse button, and drag the icon to a clear spot near the middle of the desktop.

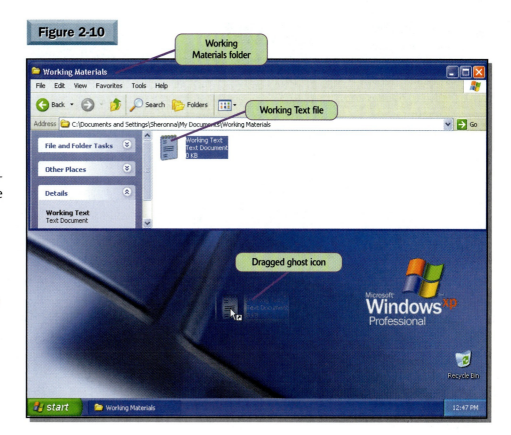

Figure 2-10

4 Release the right mouse button to reveal the shortcut menu and select **Move Here** to move the file to the desktop.

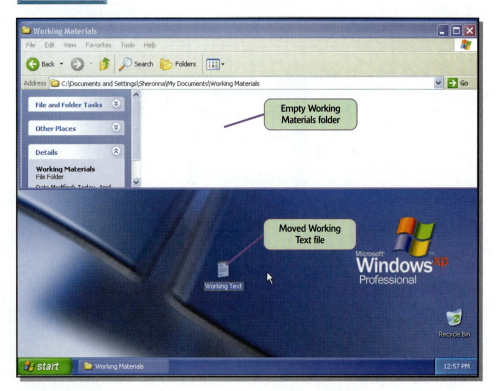

Figure 2-11

5 Select **Edit | Undo Move** to put the file back in the Working Materials folder. Then drag the **Working Text** file with the right mouse button to the desktop again, release the mouse button, and select **Copy Here**.

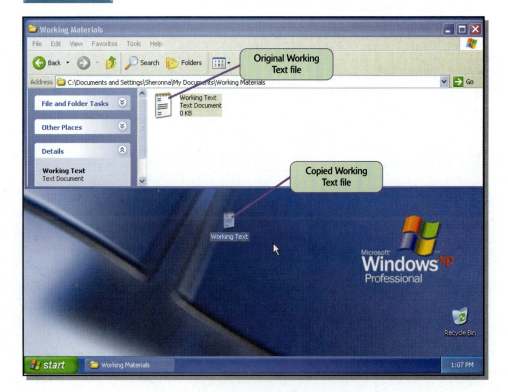

Figure 2-12

6 Right-click the **Working Text** file on the desktop, select **Rename**, type **Renamed File**, and press Enter.

7 Right-click a blank area on the desktop, select **New | Folder**, type **Moved Folder** as the folder's new name, and press Enter.

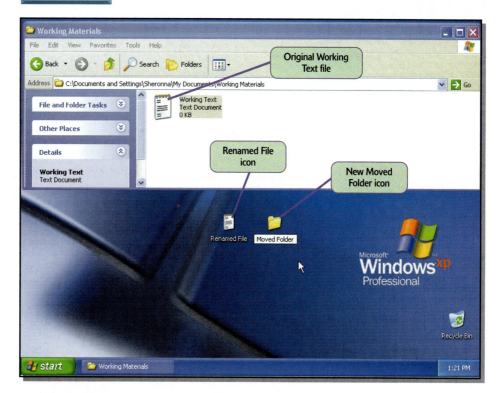

Figure 2-13

8 Drag the **Renamed File** icon on top of the **Moved Folder** icon. Then drag the **Moved Folder** icon into the opened Working Materials window to move the folder and its contents to the Working Materials folder.

9 Close the Working Materials window.

> **Tip** Notice that dragging and dropping with the left mouse button simply moves the object, whereas when using the right mouse button, you are given a shortcut menu with available choices of actions.

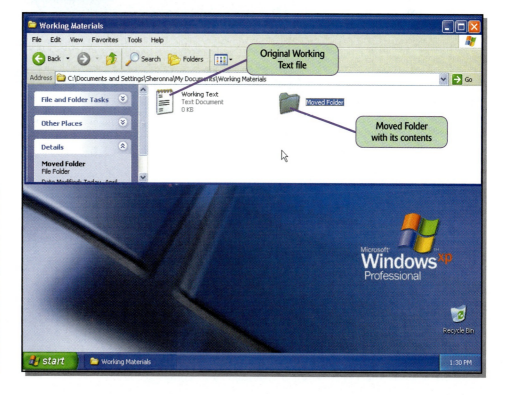

Figure 2-14

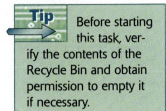

Tip Before starting this task, verify the contents of the Recycle Bin and obtain permission to empty it if necessary.

Task 4:
To Delete and Restore Files and Folders

1 Choose **Start | My Documents** to open the My Documents folder. Double-click the **Working Materials** folder that you created in Task 3.

2 Click the **Working Text** file and choose **File | Delete**.

Deleting and Restoring Files and Folders

Once you are proficient at manipulating files and folders, the likelihood that you will need to delete some of them increases. During that process, you will probably delete one that you actually need and have to restore it. In this task, you will learn how to delete files and folders as well as restore them to their former location.

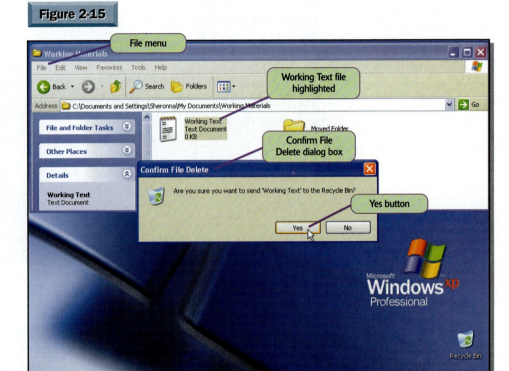

Figure 2-15

3 Click **Yes** in the Confirm File Delete dialog box; then right-click the Recycle Bin to reveal its shortcut menu.

Figure 2-16

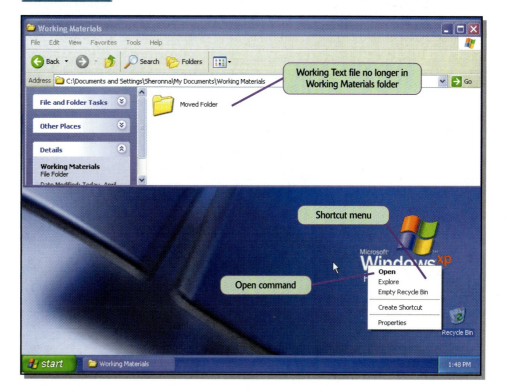

4 Select **Open** to open the Recycle Bin. Right-click a blank area on the taskbar and choose **Tile Windows Horizontally**.

5 Click the **Working Text** file and choose **File | Restore** in the Recycle Bin window. This removes the Working Text file from the Recycle Bin and restores it to the location from which it was deleted.

Figure 2-17

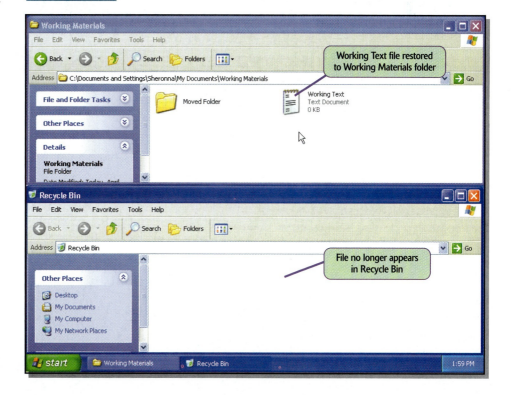

Using Files and Folders

6. Double-click the **Moved Folder** icon to open it in the same window, right-click the **Renamed File** icon, select **Delete**, and click **Yes**.

7. Click the Moved Folder window's **Back** arrow to return to the Working Materials window. Then drag the **Moved Folder** icon to the opened Recycle Bin window.

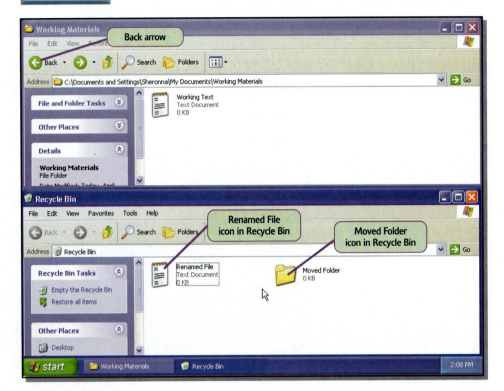

Figure 2-18

8. Click the **Renamed File** icon and choose **File | Restore** in the Recycle Bin window to return the file to its former location. Notice that the Moved Folder icon was also restored to the Working Materials folder.

9. Close the Recycle Bin. Click the **Back** arrow in the Working Materials window and drag the **Working Materials** folder to the Recycle Bin.

10. Right-click the Recycle Bin, choose **Empty Recycle Bin**, click **Yes** in the Confirm Multiple File Delete dialog box, and close the My Documents folder.

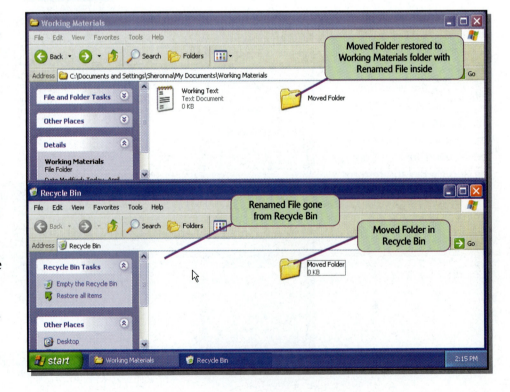

Figure 2-19

Working with Windows

Sometimes you may have to actually navigate to an item's location inside your computer. You may not know exactly what the item is called, but you do know where it is or you may want to view multiple objects along the way to the item you end up opening. In this task, you will learn to navigate through your computer with My Computer.

Task 5:
To Work with Windows

1. Choose **Start | My Computer** to open the My Computer window. Notice the information listed in the left pane and the objects displayed in the right pane.

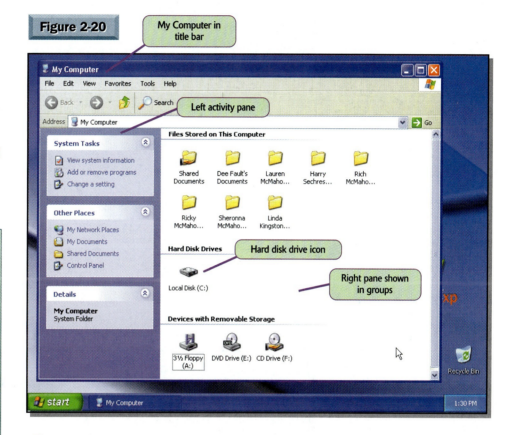

Figure 2-20

 Tip If the default settings have not been changed, the folders will each open in the same window when you double-click them. However, holding the Ctrl key down as you double-click folders reverses that particular default setting, and each successive window is left open.

Troubleshooting Your folder's settings may have your items organized in a different format than used in the example. Their organization at this point does not matter as long as you can still see that there are files stored there.

Working with Windows

2 Hold down the Ctrl key and double-click the hard disk drive icon. The contents of the hard disk drive display in a separate window (unless the default settings have been changed).

> **Troubleshooting**
>
> If you are logged in as an administrator, you will be able to access the C:\ drive files as shown. If not, you will be warned that the system files are hidden. Click **Show the contents of this folder** in the bottom of the right pane to view the files.

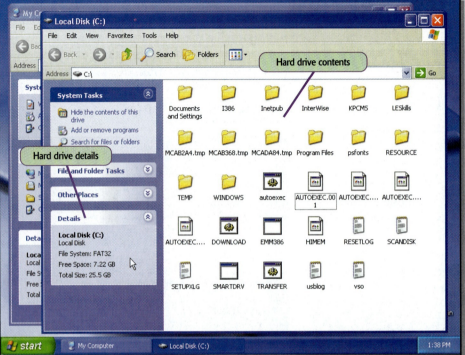

Figure 2-21

3 Hold down the Ctrl key and double-click **Documents and Settings**. The Documents and Settings folder opens in a separate window and displays the users' document folders.

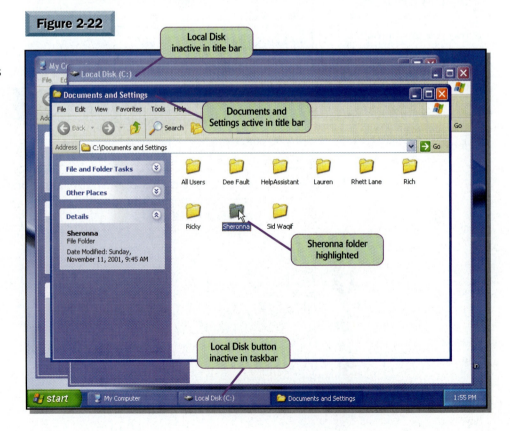

Figure 2-22

Working with Files and Folders WN 2-17

4 Hold down the Ctrl key and double-click the folder that has your user name in the Documents and Settings window. This opens your documents folder in another window.

Troubleshooting
These objects might not all be yours if your user name is shared between multiple individuals. Additionally, the files you store in these folders are accessible to anyone able to log on to that workstation.

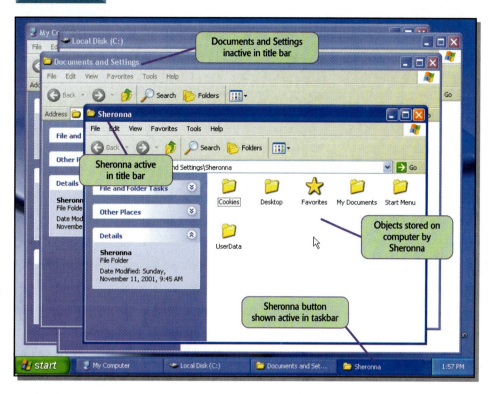

Figure 2-23

5 Hold down the Ctrl key and double-click the **My Documents** folder to display your user's stored objects in another window.

6 Hold down the Ctrl key and double-click the **My Music** folder.

7 Right-click the **Windows Explorer** button in the taskbar and select **Close Group** to close the entire group of open objects.

Troubleshooting
If the buttons are not grouped, you will have to close each folder individually or continue opening folders until grouping occurs.

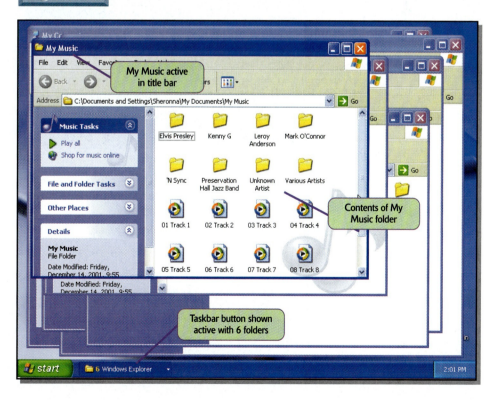

Figure 2-24

Switching Between My Computer and Windows Explorer Views

Windows gives you two alternate methods for locating items on the computer—the My Computer and Windows Explorer programs. Using My Computer provides you with object information in the left pane of the window. Opening an object using that method and switching over to the Windows Explorer view will help you understand the differences between these two programs. In this task, you will open a folder, change to the Windows Explorer view, and, while that folder remains open, navigate to the same folder with My Computer.

Task 6:
To Switch Between My Computer and Windows Explorer Views

1 Choose **Start | My Documents** to open the My Documents window.

> **Troubleshooting**
> If the window is maximized, click the **Restore** button near the right corner of the window's title bar, and resize the window, if necessary.

2 Click the **Folders** button in the toolbar to change to the Windows

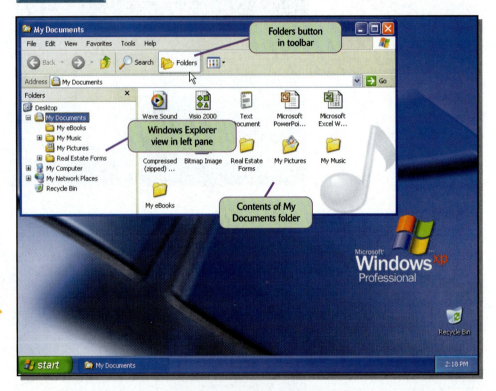

Figure 2-25

Tip Notice that the Windows Explorer navigation pane replaces the action sidebar on the left.

Working with Files and Folders WN 2-19

3 Click the **Folders** button in the toolbar again to change back to the previous view; then choose **Start | My Computer** to open My Computer in a second window.

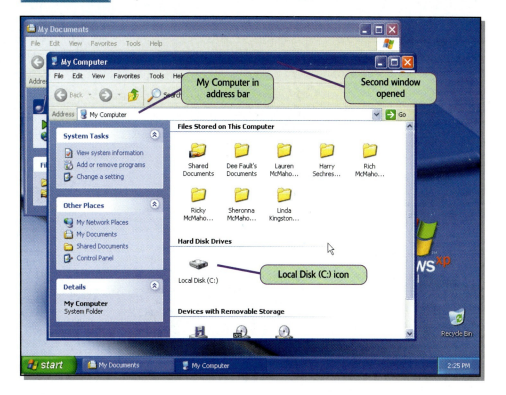

Figure 2-26

4 Double-click the **Local Disk (C:)** icon to display its contents in the same window.

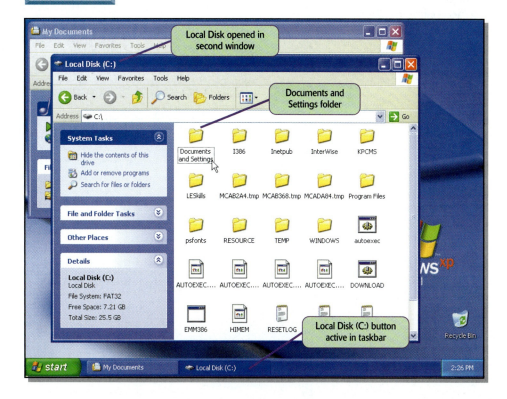

Figure 2-27

5 Double-click the **Documents and Settings** folder, double-click the folder that has your user name inside the Documents and Settings folder, and then double-click the **My Documents** folder. Each of the two open windows now displays the contents of the My Documents folder.

Tip When opening folders in the same window, you can click the **Back** button to go back to the previous window. Then you can click the **Forward** button to return to where you started.

6 Right-click a blank area on the taskbar to open its shortcut menu and view the tiling options available.

7 Click **Tile Windows Horizontally** in the shortcut menu. Compare the two windows and notice that they both display the contents of the My Documents folder.

8 Press and hold the Ctrl key down and click both **My Documents** buttons in the taskbar. Then right-click either one of the highlighted buttons and select **Close Group** to close both folders.

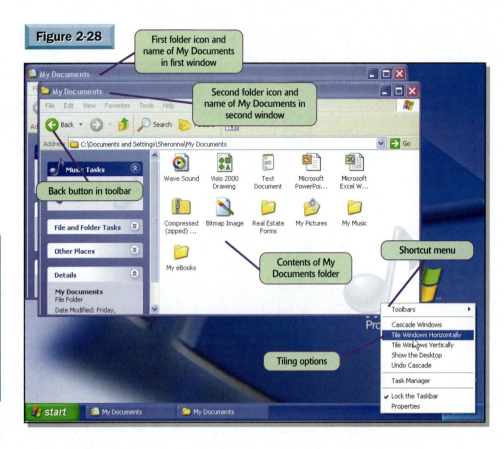

Figure 2-28

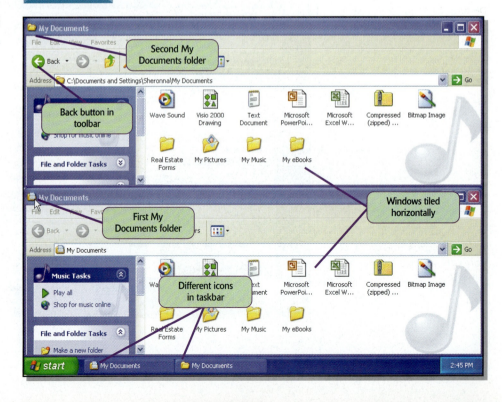

Figure 2-29

Working with Files and Folders

CHECK POINT

Remember your earlier use of the tiling function. *Tiling windows* vertically opens all windows currently on the desktop (not minimized) with equal vertical spacing. Tiling windows horizontally will open those windows with equal horizontal spacing. *Cascading windows* stacks them on top of each other (slightly offset) with the active window displayed on top.

Navigating in Windows Explorer

Windows XP emphasizes using Windows Explorer as the primary method for locating items on the computer. Windows Explorer is more intuitive than My Computer. You may find Windows Explorer easier to master, and it will more likely help keep your desktop uncluttered. In this task, you will open a folder with Windows Explorer and then navigate to other locations.

Task 7:
To Navigate in Windows Explorer

1. Choose **Start**, right-click **My Documents**, and select **Explore**. This opens the My Documents folder in Windows Explorer, with the folder expanded in the window's left navigation pane.

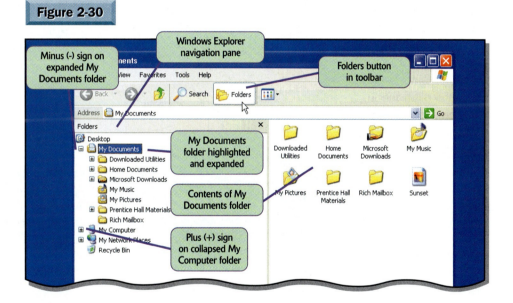

Figure 2-30

2. Pass the mouse pointer over (but do not click) My Computer in the left pane to see it change to a hyperlink.

> **Tip**
> Notice that when you point to My Computer, the text turns into a *hyperlink* (text that, if clicked, takes you to another location).

3. Click the minus (-) sign beside **My Documents** to collapse the folder; then expand (click the + sign beside) the **My Computer** folder. This displays the contents of the My Computer folder in the left navigation pane and the right contents pane.

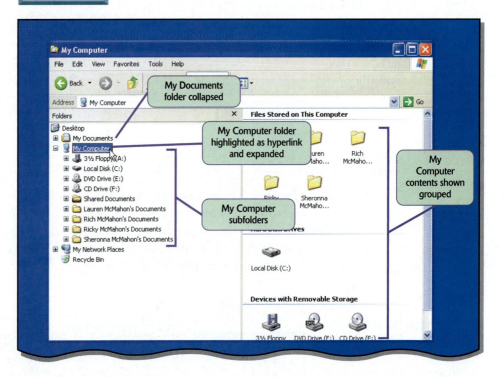

Figure 2-31

4. Click the plus (+) sign beside **My Documents** in the left pane to expand the folder; then click the **My Pictures** folder in the left pane to display its contents.

5. Click the **Close** button at the top of the left navigation pane to close the Windows Explorer view; then click the **Close** button in the title bar of the My Pictures window.

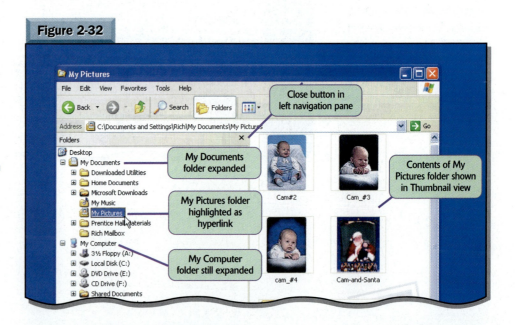

Figure 2-32

> **Tip**
> When using Windows Explorer's left navigation pane, only folders with *subfolders* (folders with other folders inside them) can be expanded. Folders with only files in them will show their contents in the right pane but cannot be expanded in the left pane.

Customizing the Start Menu

One of the main attractions of Windows XP is that it allows you to customize your environment. The Start menu is another location where you can make changes to suit your own needs. You should also know where the computer keeps track of your frequently used items and that this list of items can be modified. In this task, you are provided the opportunity (if you have permission) to make changes to the way you view the Start menu.

Task 8:
To Customize the Start Menu

1 Choose **Start**, right-click the blue space to the left of the Log Off button, and point to the **Properties** button.

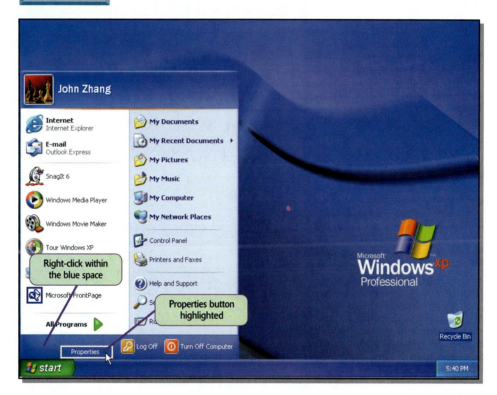

Figure 2-33

2 Click the **Properties** button to open the Taskbar and Start Menu Properties dialog box.

Figure 2-34

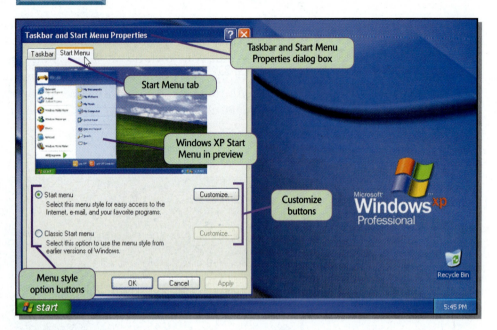

3 Click the **Classic Start menu** option button to see that style's preview.

Troubleshooting
Do not make any changes to the computer's settings unless you have permission to do so.

Figure 2-35

4 Click the **Start menu** option button to return to the Windows XP style; then click the **Customize** button to open the Customize Start Menu dialog box. Note how the Start menu can be customized using the options provided on the General tab.

Figure 2-36

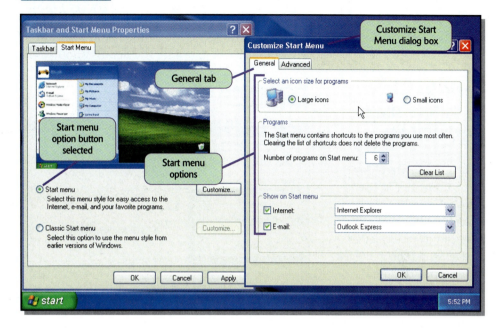

5 Click the **Advanced** tab to display the more advanced Start menu options; then use the scroll bar to scan options for viewing My Computer on the Start menu. Click **Display as a menu** so My Computer uses submenus instead of the default **Display in a link** setting.

6 Click the **Clear List** button to delete the list of your most recently opened files displayed on the Start menu. Then click the **Cancel** button twice to cancel any pending changes. (You may click the **OK** button twice to apply the changes only if you have permission to make these changes.)

Figure 2-37

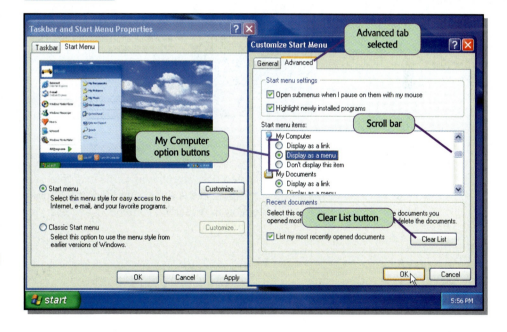

Troubleshooting
When you click the Clear List button, only the "list" of recently used files is deleted, not the "actual" files.

Other Ways

To open the My Computer folder itself and ignore the submenus, if applied:
- Choose **Start**, right-click **My Computer**, and click **Open**.
- Choose **Start**, right-click **My Computer**, and click **Explore**.

Gathering Hard Drive Details

The *Details section* in the My Computer window can be used to determine the remaining storage space available on your hard drive. In this task, you will use My Computer to examine the details about your hard drive's capacity.

Task 9:
To Gather Hard Drive Details

1. Choose **Start | My Computer** to open the My Computer window; maximize the window, if necessary. Notice whether the Details section in the left pane is open or closed.

Tip The information sections in the left pane can be individually opened or closed by clicking the arrows beside each section. The section is opened when the double arrows face upward and closed when they face downward.

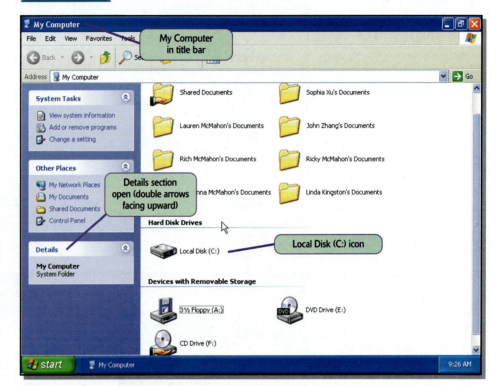

Figure 2-38

Troubleshooting Opening the My Computer folder with a limited user account (as in the example) shows a *These files are hidden* message in the right pane. Click the **Show the contents of this folder** option to reveal the contents, if necessary.

2 Double-click the **Local Disk (C:)** icon and click the **Details** section double arrows if the section is not already open. Note your file system type and determine your free space as a percentage of the total disk size (divide free space by total size and multiply by 100).

Troubleshooting
If the information sections in the left pane are all open and extend beyond the bottom of the screen, close the sections you do not need.

3 Click the **Close** button on the open window.

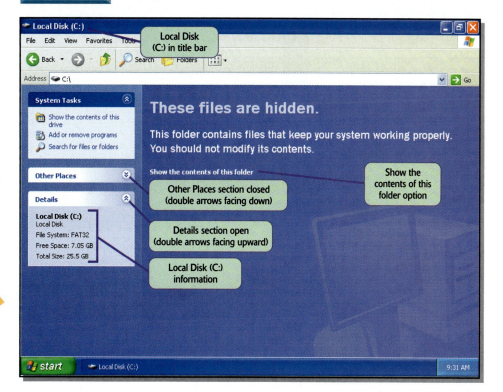

Figure 2-39

Tip Whenever the percentage of free disk space falls under 10% of the total disk space, the system's speed will be seriously degraded, and you should investigate ways of increasing the amount of available storage space on your computer.

Conducting a Basic Search

Finding objects on the computer can sometimes be challenging. Windows XP provides a feature that enables you to conduct basic searches easily. Learning how to perform a search correctly can save you significant time. In this task, you will conduct a basic search to locate a file stored on the computer.

Task 10:
To Conduct a Basic Search

1 Choose **Start | My Documents**, click **Make a new folder** in the left pane, type **Sample Documents** as the new folder's name, and press Enter.

2 Choose **File | New | Text Document**, type **Sample Document** as the name of a new document, and press Enter. Choose **File | Close** to close the My Documents window.

3 Choose **Start | Search** to open the Search Results window and point to the **All files and folders** option in the left pane.

4 Click **All files and folders** to display a section in the left pane that allows you to furnish search criteria. Type **Sample Document** into the **All or part of the file name** text box.

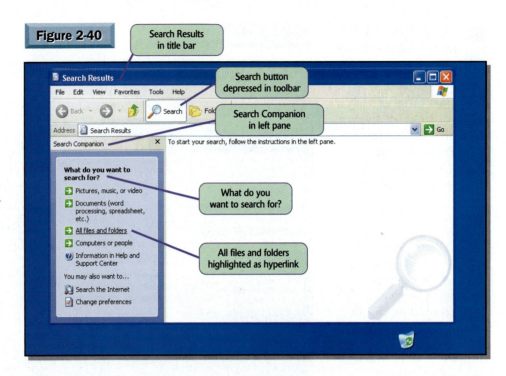

Figure 2-40

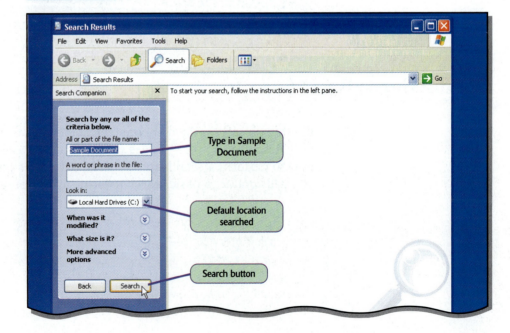

Figure 2-41

5 Click the **Search** button to locate any occurrences of the object in the default search location. Note the number of instances found and the location for each instance.

6 Click the **Close** button in the title bar to exit the Search Results window.

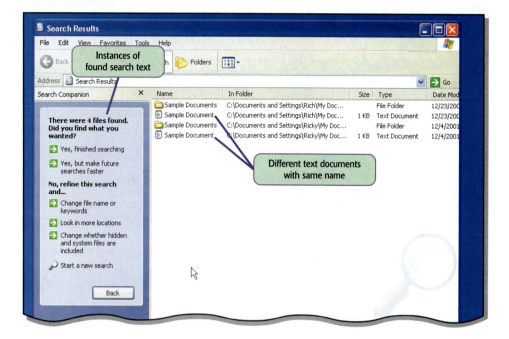

Figure 2-42

Troubleshooting You may see other items listed in the search results than those for which you are searching. For instance, the example shows another file named Sample Document (located in a different folder) in addition to two folders with the same name. The two examples of each object are different because one set is located in Rich's Documents and Settings folder and the other is located in Ricky's Documents and Settings folder.

Formatting a Floppy Disk

Much of the work that you do while using computers will typically be done on multiple workstations. Under normal circumstances, you will not be allowed to store your files on those computers. Therefore, you should always keep copies of your work. A *floppy disk* is a removable storage device that is convenient for storing those files, easy to use, and widely available. In this task, you will search for information and learn to *format* (prepare for initial use) a floppy disk.

If you are not going to need a floppy disk, you can skip this task. Otherwise, ensure that a non-write-protected, blank high density (HD) floppy disk is inserted in your computer's *floppy disk drive* (the device that reads and writes the information to floppy disks). Request your instructor's assistance if you have difficulty inserting the disk or need additional help.

Task 11:
To Format a Floppy Disk

1 Choose **Start | My Computer** and click the **3½ Floppy (A:)** icon to display the floppy disk's details in the left pane.

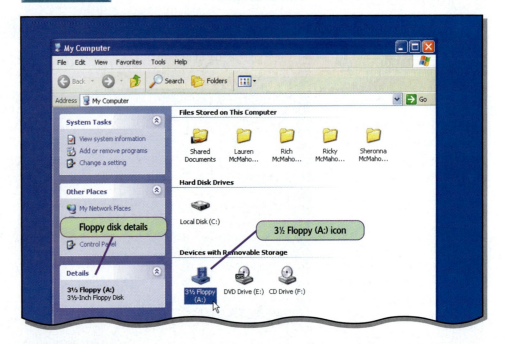

Figure 2-43

2 Right-click the **3½ Floppy (A:)** icon and select **Format** to display the Format 3½ Floppy (A:) dialog box. Type **SAMPLE** in the **Volume label** text box and leave all other default settings untouched.

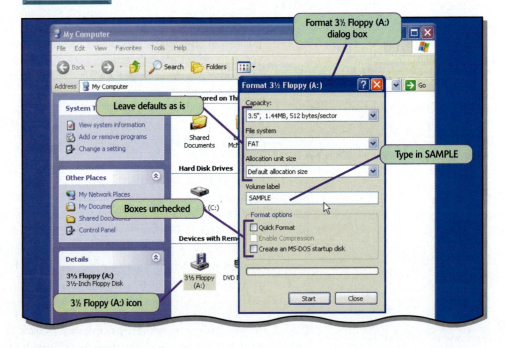

Figure 2-44

Working with Files and Folders   WN 2-31

3 Choose **Start | Help and Support** to open the Help and Support Center window.

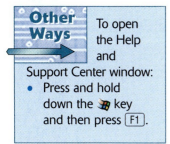

Other Ways

To open the Help and Support Center window:
• Press and hold down the ⊞ key and then press F1.

4 Type **Quick Format** in the Search box and click the green **Start searching** button to locate information about using the Quick Format feature.

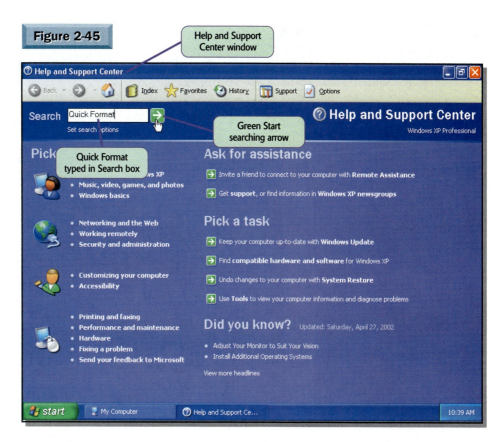

Figure 2-45

5 Click **Format a disk** in the left pane and scroll down the right pane to locate information about using the Quick Format feature. Click the **Close** button to return to the Format 3½ Floppy (A:) dialog box.

Tip

As noted in the Help and Support Center window, you should use the Quick Format feature only if the disk has been previously formatted and you are sure the disk is not damaged.

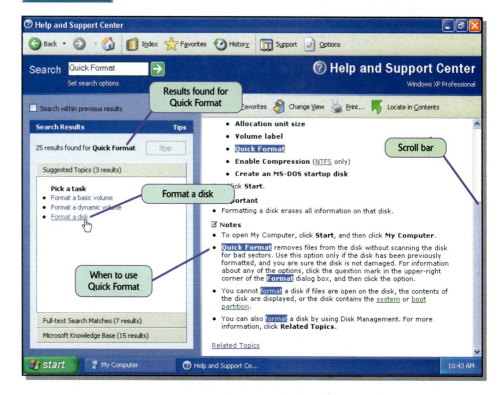

Figure 2-46

6 Click the **Start** button in the Format 3½ Floppy (A:) dialog box and click **OK** to confirm the warning and begin formatting the disk. You can observe the progress indicator near the bottom of the dialog box.

7 Click **OK** when the Formatting 3½ Floppy (A:) Format Complete dialog box appears.

8 Click the **Close** buttons on the remaining open windows.

Figure 2-47

SUMMARY AND EXERCISES

SUMMARY

- Files and folders help you organize and keep the workspace free of clutter.
- The Minimize and Maximize buttons help manage window screen size. When the Maximize button is used to display the window as a full screen, the button changes into the Restore Down button, which then can be used to return the window to its previous size.
- An active window's button is depressed in the taskbar, and its title bar is darkened. You can resize the window by pointing to an edge of the window and dragging the double-headed arrow.
- Several different views are available when inspecting the objects stored in a folder. The views available are context sensitive, and some are not always available.
- Navigating in Windows Explorer is more intuitive and easier than in My Computer. The Folders button on the toolbar allows you to switch between the two views.
- Holding the [Ctrl] key down as you double-click successive folders in windows reverses the default setting for opening windows on the computer. When opening windows in the same folder space, you can use the Forward and Back arrows on the toolbar.
- When using Windows Explorer for navigation, clicking a plus (+) sign expands the associated folder while clicking a minus (-) sign collapses it. Only folders with additional subfolders, not individual files, are displayed with a plus or minus sign next to the folder name.
- Objects can be moved or copied by dragging with either the right or left mouse button.
- Files and folders deleted and stored in the Recycle Bin can be restored to their original location.
- You can configure the Start menu using its Properties button. You can clear some of the lists that Windows XP keeps on frequently used items, such as recent files.
- The left pane displays Details on the selected object when navigating with My Computer. These details include total disk drive size and remaining disk drive space.
- Use the Search feature to help locate objects on the computer.
- Before using a floppy disk, you may have to format the disk to prepare it for use.
- Use the Help and Support Center window to locate information or tips about actions you are about to undertake.

KEY TERMS & SKILLS

KEY TERMS

cascading windows (p. 2-21)
Details section (p. 2-26)
floppy disk (p. 2-29)
floppy disk drive (p. 2-29)
format (p. 2-29)
hyperlink (p. 2-22)
Maximize/Restore Down button (p. 2-3)
Minimize button (p. 2-3)
subfolders (p. 2-22)
tiling windows (p. 2-21)
Views button (p. 2-6)

SKILLS

Change folder views in My Documents (p. 2-7)
Conduct a basic search (p. 2-28)
Customize the Start menu (p. 2-23)
Delete and restore files and folders (p. 2-12)
Format a floppy disk (p. 2-30)
Gather hard drive details (p. 2-26)
Manipulate files and folders (p. 2-9)
Navigate in Windows Explorer (p. 2-21)
Switch Between My Computer and Windows Explorer views (p. 2-18)
Use file and folder tools (p. 2-3)
Work with windows (p. 2-15)

STUDY QUESTIONS

MULTIPLE CHOICE

1. Which of the following bars is not located in the top section of a typical window in Windows XP Professional?
   a. title bar
   b. status bar
   c. toolbar
   d. menu bar

2. What action should you expect to see when you click a minimized object shown on the taskbar?
   a. The taskbar's button will appear pressed, and the object will be the active window.
   b. The Minimize button will appear, and the object will disappear from view.
   c. The object will close, and the taskbar button will disappear.
   d. The object will become maximized and will always fill the entire screen.

3. Which of the following items cannot have its location moved in a typical window?
   a. menu bar
   b. title bar
   c. toolbar
   d. address bar

4. Which of the following buttons is located immediately to the left of the red button on the title bar and serves a dual purpose?
   a. Folders/My Computer
   b. Open/Close
   c. Minimize/Maximize
   d. Maximize/Restore Down

5. Without additional customization, which of the following bars cannot be used to close an object?
   a. menu bar
   b. toolbar
   c. taskbar
   d. title bar

6. Which of the following bars contains shortcut icons for many of the actions you are able to perform with drop-down menus?
   a. title bar
   b. taskbar
   c. toolbar
   d. status bar

7. The practice of folder navigation may include all of the following except
   a. the use of subfolders.
   b. files stored in folders.
   c. folders stored in files.
   d. folders stored in folders.

8. In Windows Explorer navigation, the minus (-) sign is used to
   a. exit an application.
   b. collapse a folder.
   c. expand a folder.
   d. open an application.

9. What is the name of the window that will close if you click the red X button on the window's title bar?
   a. active window
   b. standardized window
   c. status window
   d. minimized window

10. When you want to erase all the items on a storage disk and prepare it for future use, you should
    a. put it in the Recycle Bin.
    b. format it.
    c. replace it.
    d. remove it.

SHORT ANSWER

1. Which two actions are possible when clicking the middle button on the right end of a window's title bar?
2. What does clicking the Folders button on the toolbar do?
3. When using the Windows Explorer view, what replaces the action sidebar when switching from the My Computer view?
4. By default, where does Windows XP open each folder that you double-click?
5. Where can you change some of the configuration settings for the Start menu?
6. After highlighting your C: drive's icon, which direction do the double arrows in the left pane have to face before you are able to read the details?
7. What should you do to a floppy disk prior to using it for the first time?
8. Where are objects that are currently located in a folder displayed when navigating with the Windows Explorer view?
9. What do you click, when navigating with the Windows Explorer view, to collapse other folders and expand the folder of choice?
10. Which tab of the Customize Start Menu dialog box is used to display the options necessary to change whether or not submenus are used instead of links in the My Computer and My Documents options of the Start menu?

FILL IN THE BLANK

1. A(n) _____ button in the taskbar signifies that the object is the active window.
2. The _____ button is available after clicking the Maximize button in the title bar.
3. You can resize a nonmaximized window by pausing the mouse pointer over an edge of the window and dragging the _____.
4. There are different _____ available in folder navigation that you can use to see the objects in other formats.

5. To reverse the setting used for opening folders in a window, press and hold down the _____ key while double-clicking an object.
6. Right-clicking on a button in the taskbar that represents multiple objects and selecting _____ will close all associated open objects.
7. Click the _____ in the toolbar to switch from the My Computer view to the Windows Explorer view.
8. When opening folders in the same window, you can click the _____ to navigate to a previous window.
9. To _____ a folder in the Windows Explorer view, click the minus sign.
10. Only _____ can be expanded when using the left navigation pane of the Windows Explorer view.

FOR DISCUSSION

1. Explain the two primary methods of navigating folders in Windows XP and how they differ.
2. When would you use the Quick Format feature to format a floppy disk?
3. Discuss the purpose of the search function.
4. Why is it important to understand the Help feature?
5. Explain the procedures for changing the Start menu's My Computer selection so that it uses subfolders instead of a link.

GUIDED EXERCISES

1 COPYING A NEW FOLDER AND ITS CONTENTS

Your department head has asked you to change some of the local network folder storage methods. Log on to the local computer and use the following steps to create new folders and work with your department's files.

1. Right-click a blank area of the desktop, click **New**, and then click **Folder**. Accept the default name for the folder.

2. Double-click the **New Folder** icon to open it.

3. Right-click inside the New Folder window, click **New**, and then click **Text Document**. Accept the default file name.

4. Close the New Folder window.

5. Right-click the New Folder icon, drag it to another blank area on the desktop, and then click **Copy Here**.

6. Double-click the new **Copy of New Folder** icon and notice that it also includes a copy of the New Text Document file that you had created in the original folder. Close the window.

7. Leave the folders on the desktop for the next exercise.

Working with Files and Folders　　WN 2-37

② RENAMING FILES

Your department wants several file names changed to better reflect their present use in the newly organized section where you work. Log on to the local computer and follow these steps to rename several new files:

1. Locate the New Folder and Copy of New Folder icons and their contents from Guided Exercise 1.

2. Open the Copy of New Folder folder, right-click the **New Text Document** file, and click **Rename**.

3. Type in the new name **Test Text** and press [Enter].

4. Right-click the newly renamed **Test Text** document, drag it to a blank area in the Copy of New Folder window, and click **Copy Here**. Notice that the original object remains intact when copying.

5. Click **Edit | Select All**.

6. Right-click one of the highlighted text documents and click **Rename**.

7. Type **New Text Doc** and press [Enter] to rename both documents.

8. Close all open windows and leave the folders on the desktop for the next exercise.

③ MOVING A FOLDER

Your department created and renamed several files and folders that were recently pointed out as needing to be moved to new locations to emphasize their importance in the new organization structure. Log on to the local computer and use the following steps to move several of these files and folders:

1. Locate the New Folder and Copy of New Folder icons and their contents from Guided Exercise 2.

2. Right-click the **Copy of New Folder** icon, drag it over to the **New Folder** icon, drop it in the New Folder icon, and click **Move Here**. Notice that the original object does not remain intact in a move operation. It is moved to the new location.

3. Double-click the **New Folder** icon on the desktop. Verify that the moved object (Copy of New Folder) did actually move there.

4. Double-click the **Copy of New Folder** folder in the window and verify that the contents also moved with the folder.

5. Close all open windows and leave the folder on the desktop for the next exercise.

4 DELETING AND RESTORING FILES AND FOLDERS

In the process of reorganizing the new files and folders your department needed, you collected several items that need to be discarded. Your coworkers have suggested that you should not discard anything without first knowing how to retrieve something accidentally thrown away. Log on to the local computer and use the following steps to delete objects and later restore selected files:

1. Empty the Recycle Bin to see the effects of working with it in this exercise.

2. Locate the New Folder icon with its Copy of New Folder folder and its contents from Guided Exercise 3.

3. Double-click the **New Folder** icon, right-click the **Copy of New Folder** icon, drag it over to the Recycle Bin, drop it there, and click **Move Here**. Notice that the Recycle Bin indicates that it has contents.

4. Double-click the Recycle Bin to open it and view its contents. Then right-click the taskbar and select **Tile Windows Vertically**.

5. Right-click the **Copy of New Folder** icon that you just discarded and click **Restore**.

6. Confirm that the **Copy of New Folder** icon did return to its previous location, inside the New Folder window. Close the Recycle Bin window.

7. Close the New Folder window, right-click its icon on the desktop, click the **Delete** button, and click **Yes** to confirm the folder deletion.

8. Right-click the **Recycle Bin** icon, click **Empty Recycle Bin**, and click the **Yes** button to confirm the file deletion.

ON YOUR OWN

The difficulty of these case studies varies: ⚑ are the least difficult; ⚑⚑ are more difficult; and ⚑⚑⚑ are the most difficult.

1 WORKING WITH FOLDER VIEWS

⚑ Use the Start menu to open the My Documents folder. Create a new folder and name it **Own 1 Folder**. Create a new Text Document and name it **Own 1 Text Document**. Copy that file inside the Own 1 Folder icon and name the copied file **Own 1 Text Document 2**. Use the Views button in the Own 1 Folder's toolbar to change the folder's view to the Details view and then to the List view. Determine which of these two views gives you the most information about your files.

2 CREATING A FOLDER AND FILE IN WINDOWS EXPLORER

⚑⚑ Using the Start menu, open the My Documents folder and use the Folders button to change to Windows Explorer. Add a new folder named **Own Folder 2** to the My Documents folder and a new text document file named **Own File 2**. Drag the Own File 2 from the right contents pane to the Own Folder 2 folder in the Windows Explorer left navigation pane. Open Own Folder 2 by double-clicking the folder in the left navigation pane. Right-click Own Folder 2 and delete the folder. Empty the Recycle Bin to erase the file from the computer.

3 FORMATTING A FLOPPY DISK

> Format a floppy disk and name the newly formatted disk **My Data Disk**. Move the Own 1 Folder and its contents to your new My Data Disk. Then open the disk's window, move its contents to the Recycle Bin, and notice what happens to the files.

4 WORKING WITH A FLOPPY DISK

> Empty the Recycle Bin (if it is not already empty) before beginning this exercise. Format a floppy disk and name the newly formatted disk **My Recycled Material**. Use the Start menu to open My Computer and then open the 3½ floppy disk drive. Create a new folder on the 3½ floppy disk and name it **Nonrecycled Material**. Right click the Nonrecycled Material folder and select Delete. Confirm the File Delete action and notice whether or not the folder went to the Recycle Bin.

Glossary

Active window The window in which you are currently working.

Address bar The drop-down list near the top of an object's window that can be used to access or search for resources either locally or on a network (including the Internet).

Administrative privileges Privileges necessary to control access and use that, when assigned to a user, afford the user powers to maintain computers or networks, including, for example, installing all applications and hardware items, creating and controlling all user accounts, and making changes to the system's hardware or software architecture.

Cascading windows A method of displaying open windows such that each successive window is stacked in front of the previous window (slightly offset), with the most currently opened window at the top of the stack.

Case sensitive A characteristic of passwords, whereby passwords are verified by comparing the entry against the exact combination of uppercase and lowercase letters that were used when the password was created.

Click The act of pressing and releasing the left mouse button. This action is often used to select an object or place a cursor in the intended location.

Computer administrator account The more powerful of the two local user account types in Windows XP. This account type provides the user with administrative rights to the computer.

Default configuration The initial settings that are automatically invoked when the operating system is installed. You can change many default settings to suit your own needs.

Desktop A computer's version of the top of one's desk, where you can access and run the applications on your system via program icons, buttons on the taskbar, or the Start menu.

Details section An area in the left pane of the My Computer window that can be used to determine the remaining storage space available on your hard drive.

Dialog box A small window that contains options and settings to control different objects and features.

Double-click The act of quickly pressing and releasing the left mouse button twice in succession. This action is usually used to execute an action, such as opening an application or highlighting a word in a document.

Drag To point at an object and then press and hold the mouse button down while you move the object to another location.

Floppy disk A convenient and portable object used for storing and retrieving computer data.

Floppy disk drive The mechanism used to read or write information to or from a floppy disk.

Folder An object that can be created to store other objects (including other folders) in order to organize information on the computer.

Format The action taken on a computer storage medium, such as a floppy disk, that prepares the disk to store data for future use.

Graphical User Interface (GUI) A user interface with an operating system such as Windows XP that uses pictures in addition to text in order to be more user-friendly.

Hard disk drive An internal component of your computer used for the storage of applications and files.

Hibernate To rest the computer such that all the settings and the status of your applications and open documents are saved from memory to storage on your workstation's hard disk drive.

Hotkeys The hyperlinked letters in a drop-down menu that you can use to invoke the desired menu option using the keyboard.

Hovering Holding the mouse pointer over a link or object for a few seconds to activate an informative message called a pop-up description (if one is associated with that link or object). This action is also referred to as *pausing*.

Hyperlink An item that, when clicked, sends your browser to another corresponding Web page. These items can also be used to proceed immediately from one file or location (that you have configured as a hyperlink) in a document to another file or location.

Inactive window An open window in which you are not currently working.

Limited account The more restrictive of the two local user account types in Windows XP. This account type has few administrative powers but enables the user to make changes relating to his or her own account.

Local machine The actual workstation computer where a user is working. Gaining access to the local machine refers to the ability to store objects there as opposed to storing them somewhere else on the network.

Log off The act of ending a work session on a particular computer or terminating a network connection.

Log on The act of fulfilling a computer system's security requirements to gain access to the computer or network. In Windows XP, a principal method of logging on involves clicking on the icon of a user's account and supplying a password (if one is used) to enable you to gain access to the computer.

Maximize/Restore Down button The dual-purpose button immediately to the left of the Close button in the title bar that changes depending on whether or not the object is maximized. If the object does not fill the entire desktop, you can click the Maximize button to make the object fill the desktop. Once the object does fill the desktop, that same button becomes the Restore Down button. Clicking the Restore Down button again returns the object to its original size before it was maximized.

Menu bar The horizontal bar that is typically displayed below the title bar and provides access to menu names such as File, Edit, View, Tools, and Help.

Minimize button The leftmost of the three buttons at the right end of the title bar. Clicking on that button reduces the object to a button on the taskbar.

Mouse A device attached to a computer that allows a user to point to and move objects on the desktop.

Objects Items that have properties assigned to them (such as their names). The most common objects are files and folders.

Password An arbitrary string of characters used for authenticating users and preventing unauthorized access to user accounts or computer resources.

Pausing Holding the mouse pointer over a link or object for a few seconds to activate an informative message called a pop-up description (if one is associated with that link or object). This action is sometimes referred to as *hovering*.

Point The act of moving the mouse so that the mouse pointer moves to the intended object.

Pop-up description An informational display that appears after hovering your mouse pointer over an item.

Recycle Bin An icon on the desktop that simulates the functions of a trash can. It enables the user to discard objects that are not needed, and it has the capability of retrieving discarded objects.

Restart To perform a shut down of your computer and then immediately initiate the start-up procedures without turning the computer off.

Right-click The act of pressing and releasing the right mouse button. This action is usually used to activate a context-sensitive menu, called a *shortcut menu*, that applies to the intended object.

Screen saver A feature that helps prevent images from being burned into a monitor's screen. It runs in the background without degrading or appreciably slowing down the computer's operating capability.

Scrolling Using the bars located on the right side and bottom of the screen to move a document up and down or side to side on the screen.

Shortcut menu A context-sensitive menu activated by pointing to text, a screen element, or an object and right-clicking the mouse button.

Shut down To end your current session (and all other users' current sessions) by allowing Windows XP to close all open files, store all of its operating system commands, and discard any temporary working items it has been using.

Start button A screen icon used to gain access to applications and functions on your computer. The Start button is the green button located at the left end of the taskbar.

Start menu The menu that allows the user access to the computer's applications after the Start button is clicked.

Subfolder A folder embedded within another folder.

Taskbar The horizontal bar typically displayed at the bottom of the screen and containing items such as the Start button and taskbar buttons indicating which applications are open.

Tiling windows A method of displaying open windows such that each successive window occupies the same amount of space on the desktop as the other tiled windows currently displayed.

Title bar The horizontal bar at the top of a window or dialog box that contains the control menu icon; the object's name; and the buttons such as the Minimize, Maximize/Restore Down, and Close buttons in a typical window or the Help or Close buttons in a dialog box.

Toolbar A common component of a graphical user interface that consists of a visible row of button icons. It allows the user to perform common tasks more quickly than using the menu bar.

Triple-click The act of quickly pressing and releasing the left mouse button three times in succession. This action is usually used inside text to highlight a block of text, such as a paragraph.

User account The mechanism used by the operating system to identify the personnel authorized to gain access to the workstation or the network.

Views button A toolbar button that, when available, lets you change the way you see the items displayed inside the object with which you are working.

Window The graphical view of an active object, such as an open folder, dialog box, or application.

Windows Logo key A special key recently added to the keyboards of most computers. Pressing the ⊞ key invokes shortcuts usually intended for Microsoft functionality. In particular, this key provides a quick way to activate the Start menu.

Windows Welcome screen The first screen usually encountered when logging on to a Windows XP computer. It typically shows the names of that computer's users.

Index

Symbols

… (ellipses), menu items, WN-8, WN 1-7
Ctrl key, opening windows, WN 2-15

A

active programs, identifying, WN-5
active windows, WN 1-15
address bar, Control Panel, WN-13
administrator accounts, WN 1-14
    administrative privileges, WN 1-16
    computer names, WN 1-19
    default settings, WN 1-14
All Programs list, WN-9–10
applications
    accessing via Start menu WN-8–11
    open applications on Taskbar (Taskbar buttons), WN-5, WN 2-16–17
    recent applications area, WN-8–9
Apply button (dialog boxes), WN 1-10
arrows, menu items, WN-8

B

Back button, WN 1-17
background, desktop, WN 1-3–4
basic searches, WN 2-27–29
booting the computer, WN-3–7
Browse button (dialog boxes), WN-11
buttons
    Apply (dialog boxes), WN 1-10
    Back, WN 1-17
    Clear List, WN 2-25
    Control Panel, WN 1-15
    dialog boxes, WN 1-9, WN-11
    Help, WN-11
    Log Off, WN-8
    Maximize/Minimize/Restore, WN 2-3–4
    menu bar, WN-13
    mouse, WN-12. *See also* mouse
    My Documents, WN 2-3–4
    Show the contents of this folder, WN 2-16
    shut down/turn off operations, WN 1-18–19
    Start, WN-5, WN-8
    Switch User, WN 1-18–20
    Taskbar, WN-5, WN 2-16–17
    title bar, WN 2-3–4
    Turn Off Computer, WN-8, WN-15, WN 1-20
    ungrouped, WN 2-17
    Views, WN 2-6–7

C

C:\ drive. *See* hard drives
Cancel button (dialog boxes), WN 1-9, WN 1-11–12
cascade arrows, menus, WN-8
cascading submenus, WN-11, WN-14
cascading windows, WN 2-21
case sensitivity of passwords, WN-4
clearing recently opened files list, WN 2-25
clicking (mouse action), WN-6
closing
    dialog boxes, WN 1-9
    windows, WN 1-9
commands. *See also* menus
    issuing via keystrokes, WN 1-8
    menu bar, WN-13
computer administrator accounts, WN 1-14
    administrative privileges, WN 1-16
    computer names, WN 1-19
    default settings, WN 1-14
context-sensitive menus. *See* shortcut menus
Control key, opening windows, WN 2-15
Control menu, WN-13
    closing windows, WN 2-6
    sizing windows, WN 2-4
Control Panel, WN-12
    changing mouse settings, WN-12–14
    changing user options, WN 1-15–17

Index

nouse
- name, WN 1-19
- ackground, WN 1-2–4
- lay, WN 1-8–9, WN 2-6–8
- N-12–14
- in, WN 1-10–14
- u, WN 2-23–25
- ns, WN 1-15–18

ser, WN-8
gs
- N 1-14
- ppearance, WN 2-3
- olders, WN 2-15
- in, WN 1-10, WN 1-13
- WN 1-9
- s, WN 1-9–14, WN 2-12–14.
- cycle Bin
- button, WN 2-25

e, WN 2-3
d, WN 1-3–4
N-5
n (My Computer),
27

items/tabs, WN-12–14
operties, WN 1-3–4
N-11
WN-11, WN 1-9
indows, WN-8
n Properties, WN 1-10–12

floppy disks, WN 2-29–32
s. *See* hard drives
e confirmation dialog check box
Properties dialog box),

rties dialog box, WN 1-3–4

ns list, WN-9–10
submenus, WN-10–14
enu, WN 2-4
nel, WN-12

folder contents (Show contents of this folder option), WN 2-16, WN 2-26
Start menu, WN-8–10
windows, WN 2-21
Do not move files to the Recycle Bin check box (Recycle Bin Properties dialog box), WN 1-11
dots, menu items, WN-8
double-clicking (mouse action), WN-6. *See also* mouse
    opening folders, WN 2-15
dragging items/objects, WN-6–7, WN 2-11
drives
    floppy disk, WN 2-29
    hard. *See* hard drives
drop-down list boxes (dialog boxes), WN-11
drop-down menus. *See* menus

E-F

e-mail programs, pinned area, WN-8
ellipses (...), menu items, WN-8, WN 1-7
emptying Recycle Bin, WN 1-12–13

File menu, WN 2-12
files, WN 2-2–14. *See also* **folders**
    creating, WN 1-4–7
    deleting, WN 1-10, WN 1-12
    file tools, WN 2-3–6
    hidden, WN 2-26
    highlighted file names, WN 1-5–6
    manipulating, WN 2-9–11
    naming/renaming, WN 1-5–6
    searching, WN 2-27–29
    storing, WN 1-18, WN 2-29
    viewing, WN 2-16
finding. *See* searching
floppy disks, formatting, WN 2-29–32
folders, WN 1-7–9. *See also* **files**
    active, WN 1-15
    changing views of, WN 2-6–8
    creating, WN 1-4–7
    deleting/restoring, WN 2-12–14
    folder tools, WN 2-3–6
    highlighted folder names, WN 1-5–6
    manipulating, WN 2-8–11
    open windows for each, WN 1-9

organization of, WN 2-15
searching, WN 2-27–29
settings/options, WN 1-7–9
subfolders, WN 2-22
formatting floppy disks, WN 2-29–32
free disk space, WN 2-26–27

G-H

graphical user interface (GUI), WN-5

hard drives
gathering drive details, WN 2-26–27
space, WN 1-10, WN 2-27
viewing contents, WN 2-16
Help and Support Center window, WN 2-31
Help button (dialog boxes), WN-11
Hibernate button, WN 1-18
hidden files, WN 2-26
highlighted text/objects
file names, WN 1-5–6
New Folder, WN 1-5
hotkeys, WN-12, WN 1-8
hovering, WN-6
hyperlinks, WN 2-22

I-J-K

icons
notification area, WN-5
Recycle Bin contents, WN 1-12
toolbar buttons, WN-13
identifying
active programs, WN-5
logged-in users, WN-8
inactive windows, WN 1-16

keystrokes, issuing commands. *See* **hotkeys**

L

laptop computers, WN 1-18
launching programs, WN-8
left-handed mouse users, WN-12
lists, changing sort orders, WN-9
local machine, WN 1-10
locating items. *See* **searching**

Log Off Windows button, WN-8
logging off Windows XP, WN-14–15, WN 1-18
Log Off /Turn Off Computer buttons, WN-8
logging on Windows XP, WN-3–7
users
current, WN-8
new, WN 1-20

M

maximizing windows, WN 2-3–4
menu bar, WN-13
menus
accessing commands, WN-13
hotkeys, WN-12, WN 1-8
cascading, WN-8
choosing, WN 1-8
ellipses, WN-8, WN 1-7
File, WN 2-12
shortcut. *See* shortcut menus
Start. *See* Start menu
Tools, WN 1-8
Views, WN 2-7–8
minimizing windows, WN 2-3–4
mouse
actions, WN-6
changing settings, WN-12–14
dragging/dropping, WN-6–7, WN 2-11
using on the desktop, WN-5–8
My Computer
Details section, WN 2-26–27
switching between My Computer/Windows Explorer, WN 2-18–21
working with windows, 2-15–17
My Documents, WN 2-3–6
changing views, WN 2-6–8
manipulating files/folders, WN 2-8–11

N

naming files/folders, WN 1-5–6
navigating in Windows Explorer, WN 2-21–22
switching between My Computer/Windows Explorer, WN 2-18–21
new files/folders, WN 1-4–7
notification area (Taskbar), WN-5

O

objects. *See also* files; folders
   deleting, WN 1-9–14, WN 2-12–14. *See also* Recycle Bin
      Clear List button, WN 2-25
   finding, WN 2-27–29
   opening, WN 1-20, WN 2-18
OK button (dialog boxes), WN-11, WN 1-9
opening. *See also* displaying
   dialog boxes, WN-14
   folders, WN-8
   objects, WN 1-20, WN 2-18
Option button (dialog boxes), WN-11
options. *See* customizing; settings

P-Q

passwords, WN-2
   case sensitivity, WN-4
   entering, WN-3–4
pictures of logged-in user, WN-8–9
pinned area (Start menu), WN-8
pointing the cursor, WN-6. *See also* mouse
pop-up descriptions, WN-6
power-off symbol, WN-8
programs
   All Programs list, WN-9–10
   identifying active, WN-5
   launching, WN-8
   pinned area, WN-8

Quick Format feature, WN 2-31

R

recent applications area, WN-8
Recycle Bin, WN-4–5
   changing settings, WN 1-10–14
   deleting/restoring items, WN 1-12–14
   keeping items in, WN 1-14
removable storage devices, WN 2-29
renaming files/folders, WN 1-5–6
resizing windows, WN 2-3–4
Restart button, WN 1-18

Restore Defaults button (Folder Options dialog box), WN 1-9
restoring Recycle Bin items, WN 1-12–14
   deleted folders, WN 2-12–14
restoring windows, WN 2-4, WN 2-18
right mouse button, WN-6, WN 1-5, WN 2-11

S

screen savers, WN-3
scroll bars/scrolling, WN 1-17
searches, WN 2-27–29
separator lines in menus, WN-8
settings
   default settings
      altering, WN 1-14
      desktop appearance, WN 2-3
      opening folders, WN 2-15
      Recycle Bin, WN 1-10, WN 1-13
      restoring, WN 1-9
   files/folders. *See* files; folders
   mouse, WN-12–14
   Recycle Bin, WN 1-10–14
shortcut menus, WN-6
   activating, WN-6
   closing, WN-7
   deleting folders, WN 1-13
   moving files, WN 2-10
   Recycle Bin properties, WN 1-10
   renaming files, WN 2-11
   taskbar settings, WN-7, WN 2-20
   tiling windows, WN 2-13, WN 2-20
Show contents of this folder option, WN 2-16, WN 2-26
shutting down, WN-14–15, WN 1-18–20
   Log Off /Turn Off Computer buttons, WN-8
sizing windows, WN 2-3–4
spin boxes (dialog boxes), WN-11
Stand By (hibernate) mode, WN 1-18
Start button, WN-5, WN-8
Start menu
   changing user options, WN 1-15
   customizing, WN 2-23–25
   displaying, WN-8–10
   features, WN-8, WN-11
   logging off Windows XP, WN 1-19–20

storage
    of files when shutting down the computer, WN 1-18
    Recycle Bin, WN 1-10
    removable devices for, WN 2-29
    temporary, WN 1-10
subfolders, WN 2-22
submenus, WN-8, WN-10–14
switching users, WN 1-18–20

T

tabs (dialog boxes), WN-14
Taskbar, WN-5
    notification area, WN-5
    shortcut menu, WN-7, WN 2-20
    Taskbar buttons, WN-5, WN 2-16–17
tiling windows, WN 2-13, WN 2-21
title bars (windows), WN 2-4, WN 2-11, WN 2-13
toolbar buttons (icons), WN-13
Tools menu, WN 1-8
trash can. *See* Recycle Bin
triple-clicking (mouse action), WN-6
turning off computer, WN-14–15, WN 1-18–20
    Log Off/Turn Off Computer buttons, WN-8
turning on computer, WN-2–7

U-V

users
    changing user options, WN 1-14–18
    switching, WN 1-18–20

user accounts, WN-2, WN 1-14
user names, WN-8
    altering, WN 1-14
    shared, WN 2-17
User picture, WN-8

views, WN 2-6–8
    switching between My Computer and Windows Explorer, WN 2-18–21
Views button, WN 2-6–7

W-X-Y-Z

waking the computer, WN-3
wallpaper, WN 1-4. *See also* **desktop**
windows, WN 2-15–17
    active, WN 1-15
    cascading, WN 2-21
    closing, WN 1-9
    inactive, WN 1-16
    objects as, WN 1-4
    open folder, WN 1-9
    sizing/resizing, WN 2-3–4
    tiling, WN 2-13, WN 2-21
Windows Explorer, WN 2-18–21
    navigating, WN 2-21–22
Windows Logo key, WN-9
Windows Welcome screen, WN-3
Windows XP
    desktop features, WN-5
    logging off, WN-14–15
    logging on, WN-3–7
    shutting down, WN 1-18
    Start menu. *See* Start menu